TAXATIC..
IN THE NEW STATE

WITH AN ESSAY FROM
Mark Twain's Speeches
BY MARK TWAIN

By

J. A. HOBSON

First published in 1920

British Library Cataloguing-in-Publication Data
A catalogue record for this book is available
from the British Library

TAXES AND MORALS

ADDRESS DELIVERED
IN NEW YORK, JANUARY 22, 1906

AN ESSAY FROM
Mark Twain's Speeches
BY MARK TWAIN

At the twenty-fifth anniversary of the founding of Tuskeegee Institute by Booker Washington, Mr. Choate presided, and in introducing Mr. Clemens made fun of him because he made play his work, and that when he worked hardest he did so lying in bed.

I came here in the responsible capacity of policeman to watch Mr. Choate. This is an occasion of grave and serious importance, and it seems necessary for me to be present, so that if he tried to work off any statement that required correction, reduction, refutation, or exposure, there would be a tried friend of the public to protect the house. He has not made one statement whose veracity fails to tally exactly with my own standard. I have never seen a person improve so. This makes me thankful and proud of a country that can produce such men—two such men. And all in the same country. We can't be with you always; we are passing away, and then—well, everything will have to stop, I reckon. It is a sad thought. But in spirit I shall still be with you. Choate, too—if he can.

Every born American among the eighty millions, let his creed or destitution of creed be what it may, is indisputably a

Christian—to this degree that his moral constitution is Christian.

There are two kinds of Christian morals, one private and the other public. These two are so distinct, so unrelated, that they are no more akin to each other than are archangels and politicians. During three hundred and sixty-three days in the year the American citizen is true to his Christian private morals, and keeps undefiled the nation's character at its best and highest; then in the other two days of the year he leaves his Christian private morals at home and carries his Christian public morals to the tax office and the polls, and does the best he can to damage and undo his whole year's faithful and righteous work. Without a blush he will vote for an unclean boss if that boss is his party's Moses, without compunction he will vote against the best man in the whole land if he is on the other ticket. Every year in a number of cities and States he helps put corrupt men in office, whereas if he would but throw away his Christian public morals, and carry his Christian private morals to the polls, he could promptly purify the public service and make the possession of office a high and honorable distinction.

Once a year he lays aside his Christian private morals and hires a ferry-boat and piles up his bonds in a warehouse in New Jersey for three days, and gets out his Christian public morals and goes to the tax office and holds up his hands and swears he wishes he may never—never if he's got a cent in the world, so help him. The next day the list appears in the papers—a column and a quarter of names, in fine print, and every man in the list a billionaire and member of a couple of churches. I know all those people. I have friendly, social, and criminal relations with the whole lot of them. They never miss a sermon when they are so's to be around, and they never miss swearing-off day, whether they are so's to be around or not.

I used to be an honest man. I am crumbling. No—I have crumbled. When they assessed me at $75,000 a fortnight ago I went out and tried to borrow the money, and couldn't; then when I found they were letting a whole crop of millionaires live in New York at a third of the price they were charging me I was hurt, I was indignant, and said: "This is the last feather. I am not going to run this town all by myself." In that moment—in that memorable moment—I began to crumble. In fifteen minutes the disintegration was complete. In fifteen minutes I had become just a mere moral sand-pile; and I lifted up my hand along with those seasoned and experienced deacons and swore off every rag of personal property I've got in the world, clear down to cork leg, glass eye, and what is left of my wig.

Those tax officers were moved; they were profoundly moved. They had long been accustomed to seeing hardened old grafters act like that, and they could endure the spectacle; but they were expecting better things of me, a chartered, professional moralist, and they were saddened.

I fell visibly in their respect and esteem, and I should have fallen in my own, except that I had already struck bottom, and there wasn't any place to fall to.

At Tuskeegee they will jump to misleading conclusions from insufficient evidence, along with Doctor Parkhurst, and they will deceive the student with the superstition that no gentleman ever swears.

Look at those good millionaires; aren't they gentlemen? Well, they swear. Only once in a year, maybe, but there's enough bulk to it to make up for the lost time. And do they lose anything by it? No, they don't; they save enough in three minutes to support the family seven years. When they swear, do we shudder? No—unless they say "damn!" Then we do. It shrivels us all up. Yet we ought not to feel so about it, because we all swear—everybody. Including the ladies. Including Doctor Parkhurst, that strong and brave and excellent citizen, but superficially educated.

For it is not the word that is the sin, it is the spirit back of the word. When an irritated lady says "oh!" the spirit back of it is "damn!" and that is the way it is going to be recorded against her. It always makes me so sorry when I hear a lady swear like that. But if she says "damn," and says it in an amiable, nice way, it isn't going to be recorded at all.

The idea that no gentleman ever swears is all wrong; he can swear and still be a gentleman if he does it in a nice and, benevolent and affectionate way. The historian, John Fiske, whom I knew well and loved, was a spotless and most noble and upright Christian gentleman, and yet he swore once. Not exactly that, maybe; still, he—but I will tell you about it.

One day, when he was deeply immersed in his work, his wife came in, much moved and profoundly distressed, and said: "I am sorry to disturb you, John, but I must, for this is a serious matter, and needs to be attended to at once."

Then, lamenting, she brought a grave accusation against their little son. She said: "He has been saying his Aunt Mary is a fool and his Aunt Martha is a damned fool." Mr. Fiske reflected upon the matter a minute, then said: "Oh, well, it's about the distinction I should make between them myself."

Mr. Washington, I beg you to convey these teachings to your great and prosperous and most beneficent educational institution, and add them to the prodigal mental and moral riches wherewith you equip your fortunate proteges for the struggle of life.

PREFACE

Even before the war the growing need of large revenue in order to meet the new demands upon the modern State was bringing the problem of taxation into a place of increased prominence in the politics of every civilized nation. Non-remunerative State services were continually increasing in number, scope, and intricacy, and the annual bills kept mounting up. In some countries the increased expenditure could be largely met out of income from public properties or remunerative services. But in Great Britain and in other countries the pressure for increased tax revenue was strongly felt; and new sources of this revenue were being explored. The war, with its legacies of indebtedness and its large sudden demands of State expenditure for reconstruction, must force every intelligent citizen to consider closely how a tax-income, at least three or four times as large as the pre-war sum, can best be raised. It will be evident at once that no multiplication of minor devices can suffice, but that a thorough exploration of the taxable resources of the nation must be undertaken.

These chapters are an attempt to establish and apply to the financial situation in front of us certain intelligible principles of tax policy. Recognizing that the normal annual tax-income can only be derived from the incomes of the several members of the nation, and consists of a portion of the wealth constituting the annual product of the nation reckoned in money or in goods and services, we are confronted first with the necessity of distinguishing the portions of personal incomes that have ability to bear taxation from those that have not such ability.

I have made it my first object to win, by means of a brief analysis of the various elements in income, a clear definition of 'ability to bear.' While there is nothing novel in the distinction which I draw between 'costs' and 'surplus,' I am convinced that neither in the theory nor the practice of taxation has this distinction been adequately realized. Though modern State finance has been moving empirically towards a recognition of the fundamental truth that only surplus income, *i.e.* economically unnecessary payments to owners of some factor of production, possesses a true 'ability to bear,' economists and statesmen alike still cling to the looser and defective statement of this principle conveyed in the first of Adam Smith's four maxims of taxation. That maxim declares that "The subject of every State ought to contribute towards the support of the government, as nearly as possible, in proportion to their respective abilities; that is, in proportion to their revenue which they respectively enjoy under the protection of the State."

Now, theory and practice alike attest the need of amending this maxim by a recognition that such parts of the revenue of any one as are physically or morally necessary to evoke and maintain the output of productive power which serves to create this revenue, should be excluded from the purview of this test as possessing no ability to bear taxation. All taxes which fall directly or indirectly upon this part of revenue are bad taxes, impairing the sources of production if they are borne, and causing waste and confusion if, as will usually happen, they are shifted on to some surplus element of revenue.

But while it is not difficult to establish in general terms the justice and utility of confining taxation to surplus elements of income, the difficulty or impossibility of accurately ascertaining and measuring such surpluses as they emerge in the intricacies of actual industry and commerce compels State financiers to have recourse to less direct expedients for the application of their principles. Alike in the case of the immediate taxation of income and of the deferred taxation of accumulated income through Death Duties, the two chief instruments of revenue for the modern State, the assumption is adopted that surplus wealth with 'ability to bear' varies directly with the size of the income or the estate. Our Income-Tax is thus in main outline conformable to the distinction here made between costs and surplus. The exemption limit with allowances asserts the principle that a small necessary income has no ability to bear taxation, while the progressive graduation assumes that ability rises proportionably with the dimensions of the taxable body.

But, in order to make this method of taxation thoroughly effective, certain reforms are needed. Exempted income should evidently have regard to the number of those who depend upon it for their maintenance, and progressive graduation should be more continuous and more progressive. Proposals for achieving these reforms are discussed.

Indirect taxes are generally worse than worthless for purposes of revenue, producing little, costing much, and interfering with the general productivity of industry and commerce. In the few cases where it is desirable to retain them, considerations not of revenue, but of public order, health, or the prevention of extravagance and waste determine their retention. A tariff on imports is found to be peculiarly injurious in its incidence and shifting, for it can never be directed so as to make the foreigners pay any proportion of the tax sufficient to compensate the injuries which it inflicts upon home industries and real income.

In the first part of this volume these principles and policies of reformed taxation are set out in their general bearings. The second part treats of the financial emergency in which the State must find itself as soon as the war-borrowing ceases and annual expenditure must be met out of annual revenue. The difficulties and dangers of attempting to find the required revenue by any ordinary processes of annual taxation are discussed, and it is urged that an emergency levy upon capital is requisite in order to effect such a reduction of war-indebtedness as will bring the annual revenue within the compass of safe taxation. Two proposals for a levy are described, one confined to war-made wealth, the other of a general character, and the respective merits and defects of the two are discussed. A concluding chapter deals with the adjustments between national and local taxation demanded by the application of the principle of 'ability to bear' to local services, if there is to be effective and economical co-operation of national and local government in the performance of the services and the provision of the money expended on them.

I wish to express my deep indebtedness to Mr Sidney Webb for valuable aid rendered in the preparation and correction of this work.

J. A. HOBSON

HAMPSTEAD
May 1919

CONTENTS

PART I

PRINCIPLES OF TAX REFORM

CHAP.

I. ABILITY TO PAY 3

II. THE TAXABLE SURPLUS 12

III. THE SHIFTING OF TAXES 45

IV. THE TAXATION OF INCOME 78

V. REFORMS OF INCOME-TAX 95

VI. DEATH DUTIES 110

VII. SUPPLEMENTARY TAXES 118

VIII. TARIFFS FOR REVENUE 127

PART II

EMERGENCY FINANCE

CHAP.   PAGE

I. OUR FINANCIAL EMERGENCY 145

II. A LEVY ON WAR-MADE WEALTH . . . 165
    APPENDIX. TAXATION OF WAR-MADE CAPI-
    TAL IN GERMANY 187

III. A GENERAL LEVY UPON CAPITAL . . . 189

IV. RELATIONS OF IMPERIAL TO LOCAL TAXA-
    TION 228

TAXATION IN THE NEW STATE

PART I
PRINCIPLES OF TAX REFORM

CHAPTER I

ABILITY TO PAY

§ 1. Every modern State needs a rapidly increasing revenue in order to undertake new expensive public services or to improve old ones. Some of these increasing revenues may be got from the annual yield of public properties or services. Where, as in Germany, the State has been the owner of railways and canals, large forests and mines, as well as the postal, telegraphic and other remunerative businesses, the rents and profits derived from these sources may defray in large part the cost of the non-remunerative services, such as defence, police, public health and education. If the British State can acquire upon reasonable terms and operate or lease advantageously our railways, mines, electric plant and certain other services and industries hitherto left to private enterprise, it is possible that we too may derive a large part of our State and municipal revenues from such remunerative sources. But our present situation, in which the Post Office is the only large self-supporting and profit-earning branch of our Central Government, is one which forces us to look to tax revenues as the effective sources for meeting the enormous increase of State expenditure that immediately confronts us. No close forecast of the amount of tax revenue required is relevant to my present task. It may suffice to remind readers that, unless some emergency levy sensibly reduces the burden of war debt, the interest and sinking fund upon our national debt alone will for a good many years to come be nearly double the amount of our total pre-war revenue from all sources. To this must be added a large provision for war pensions, hospitals, land settlements, training schools and industrial equipment for injured soldiers. Large necessary commitments have been made for public expenditure on housing, health and education, roads and afforestation. Unremunerative public works or other contributions towards unemployed insurance, at any rate during the period called 'reconstruction,' will probably form a considerable item of expense. Many of the war 'controls' must probably be retained either temporarily or permanently, and all departments of the civil government, enlarged in staff and functions for the duration of the war, will struggle not unsuccessfully against 'cutting down.' Thus the State will remain a much bigger body to support after the war than before. And the expense of keeping it will have expanded almost automatically to meet the rise of prices and the consequent increase in cost of living. For there is no likelihood of such a fall of prices for a long time to come as to bring salaries and wages down to anything approaching the pre-war level. An increased expenditure of 25 per cent. from this source is a low estimate.

§ 2. These considerations make it evident that our State must provide itself with a tax revenue enormously exceeding the amount, approximately 165 millions, provided by the 1913-14 Budget. Until the burden of the debt is considerably reduced, it looks as if the tax revenue must be at least four times as large as the pre-war amount. This alarming statement should, of course, be mitigated by the reflection that the monetary sources of tax revenue, money incomes and values of capital, will be found to have risen along with the rises in price-levels, though not to a corresponding extent. Thus there will be a considerable increase in the monetary size of the taxable body of wealth.

At the same time the necessary revenue will be so great as to bring issues of tax-policy into the forefront of practical politics, and to compel officials and politicians and the general public to bestow a far greater attention than hitherto upon methods of taxation. At a time when industry and commerce, dislocated by the war, are exposed to all the risks and difficulties of reconstruction, under new conditions of national and world markets, coping with various shortages of materials and transport, and subjected to new forms of State and inter-State control, all enlargements of existing taxes and all experiments in new taxation, with their intricate reactions, will be matters of grave concern to the business classes and to the workers whose wages and employment are affected. Before the war the irregularities and inequalities of the income-tax evoked some grumbling, but the toll was seldom felt to be oppressive. The post-war income-tax must be so heavy as to convert these moderate discontents into clamorous grievances. The propertied classes will be confronted with demands from the State which they will be certain to denounce as confiscation, unjust in itself and crippling to business enterprise. Every class in the community will be concerned to defend itself against taxation which seems to it excessive, and to make alternative proposals for shifting as much of it as possible on to others.

§ 3. No issue will more certainly sharpen class feeling and inflame political passion unless sane counsels prevail and intelligible rules of equity and sound economy for taxation gain general acceptance. But to establish such general rules, and win for them a general acceptance, is no easy matter. For our taxing system has grown up in the same atmosphere of groping empiricism as our other governmental institutions. It has been the off-spring of expediency and passing opportunity, not of clearly recognized and consistently applied principles of fiscal theory. Even that chief instrument of modern taxation, the income-tax, first adopted as an emergency measure in the French war at the end of the eighteenth century, was only firmly embedded in our fiscal system as a permanency half a century ago, and the predominant position which it now occupies is a more recent acquisition. The same is true of the other taxing measure next in productivity, the 'Death

Duties.' Not until the increase and graduation of these inheritance taxes in Sir William Harcourt's Budget of 1894 was the importance of this great source of revenue established. Historical investigation can, indeed, trace certain guiding principles, or general tendencies, in the development of State-taxing systems, both in this country and in the whole civilized world. In most modern States the tendency has been to draw an increasing proportion of the tax revenue from direct taxes, signifying by this term a tax demanded from a person which he is presumed to have to bear out of his own resources and to be unable to shift on to anybody else's shoulders. In not a few modern States, however, this tendency has been countered in recent times by the adoption of a high protective tariff upon imports, the real incidence of which is not deemed either by its upholders or opponents to fall wholly or mainly upon the persons who pay the duties to the customs officers. In certain sparsely peopled or chiefly agricultural communities the practical difficulties of assessment and collection have also favoured the retention of indirect taxation. But the general trend, especially in popularly governed States, has been to collect an increasing share of the revenue by direct taxation. A second and related tendency has been to do away with those specific taxes, earmarked for some special public service, which characterized the early fiscal system of most countries and which still largely survive in our municipal and county rating systems. Convenience and elasticity of expenditure in the modern State are in such strong conflict with the specific tax that this method of taxation has virtually disappeared, leaving the State full liberty to dispose of its whole revenue according to its annual estimate of its several requirements. The application of the policy of graduation to many modern taxes is also a world-wide tendency, indicating a general acceptance of a particular interpretation of the economic and ethical maxim that taxation should be levied in accordance with ability to pay.

§ 4. Accepting ability to pay as the supreme canon of economy and equity, I shall direct my inquiry to a detailed consideration of the validity of various proposals for the application of this test. But it is first essential to recognize precisely what the process called taxation does with the money that is paid to the State by the taxpayer. The revenue which our State takes by taxation during the year, its income, is expended during the year in what we may term public consumption. It goes for the payment of wages and salaries and pensions of the persons employed by the State in the military, naval and civil services, for the purchase and consumption during the year of stores, tools and other equipment demanded by these services, including considerable outlays in buildings such as ships, barracks, hospitals, arsenals, docks, roads and other works of repair or development. A not inconsiderable proportion of this whole annual expenditure goes into objects of future productive utility such as would rightly rank under capital expenditure. What taxation does, then, is to take certain portions of the income of private citizens which they would have spent or saved and to hand it over to the State to spend or save. It is of importance clearly to recognize that virtually the whole of taxation is deducted from the current income of the taxpayers. Even if it be assessed and imposed upon capital, it is almost entirely paid out of income. Where provision has been made beforehand for payment of Death Duties by insurance, this, of course, is evident. But even where it is permissible to pay Death Duties or other taxes in Government bonds or other scrip transferring capital ownership, the result is the same. For, when the State converts these capital values into cash by

putting them on the market, the proceeds represent current income of the purchasers.

Even the case of a special levy upon capital is
only exceptional in so far as it is paid, not out
of current income, but in securities which are not
put upon the market by the Government but are
held as a public property. Such a levy, however,
stands outside the normal process of taxation for
State revenue which we are now examining, and
will be left for separate consideration. It does
not impair the validity of the rule that all taxes
in the last resort are transfers of income from
individual citizens to the State. The *basis* of taxation may often be land, capital values of various
sorts, or capitalized earning power of individuals,
as in a capitation tax, but the incidence of the tax
is in all cases upon some form of money income,
or real income. In a modern State it is always a
transfer of spending or saving power from individuals to the State.

§ 5. This gives us the true starting point in our
interpretation of the canon of 'ability to pay' as
the criterion of sound taxation. Before, however,
we proceed to examine the different elements of
income in order to discover how much, if any,
'ability to pay' they severally possess, it may be
well to state in advance two basic considerations

which must guide us in our task, the full significance of which will only appear when our analysis
of income in respect of taxability has been completed.

A sound tax must conform to two negative conditions, which will be found vitally connected with
one another:

(1) It must not remove or impair any instru-
     ment of, or incentive to, essential or use-
     ful processes of production.

(2) It must not remove or impair any essential
     or useful element of consumption.

In other words, the really taxable elements of
income, those which have a true 'ability to bear'
taxation, must be those that are unnecessary to
maintain or promote socially serviceable processes
of production or consumption. The one condition
relates to the origins or sources of income, the
other to the uses to which income is applied.

CHAPTER II

THE TAXABLE SURPLUS

§ 1. In any investigation of taxation in its bearing upon the different sources or kinds of income
we cannot avoid discussing the problems of the

shifting and incidence of the various taxes. For in testing the validity and utility of each tax we must have a clear idea, first of the element of income upon which a given tax finally settles, or the person who really pays, and secondly, of the disturbances and damages it may cause in the 'shifting' process which may occur before the final settlement is reached.

Economic theory presents a sharp division between the kinds or sources of income which are in this sense taxable and those which are not, though many practical difficulties, as we shall recognize, beset the application of the theory. All incomes, apart from pensions or certain other fixed allowances, are payments to the owners of some requisite of production in respect of the services rendered by that requisite to the actual production of wealth. Or, put in another way, the monetary value of all goods or services that are produced and sold, after provision has been made for the maintenance and repair of plant, materials and other elements of the capital fabric, is distributed in various proportions as income to the capitalists, workers, landowners, business men, professional men, whose personal activities or property help to produce this wealth. The wealth itself is real income; the price of it, broken up into various payments to owners of the factors of production, is money income. Much of this income is physically and morally necessary to secure the continued use of the factor of production whose owner receives it. The workers in industry cannot go on working unless a certain wage, enabling them to repair the physical energy they have given out, is continuously paid to them. Nor is it enough that the actual workers at any given time are thus maintained. The subsistence wage must not only keep existing labour in physical efficiency, it must provide for a constant flow of young labour into the industry to take the place of those fallen out from declining powers or death. This does not, of course, necessarily mean that a subsistence wage for an individual worker, or even the standard wage in a particular trade, must be enough to enable him to keep a wife and bring up a family. For there is no physical or moral compulsion to force a worker to provide a substitute for himself when he falls out. Nor is it the case that the cost of bringing up a family to maturity must necessarily be borne by the wages of a single worker. Moreover, few industries are recruited entirely from the families of their own members. Rapidly growing industries will naturally draw their increased supply largely from industries that are declining, or of slow growth. It is only true of industry in general that the family income, to which both parents and during certain periods of family life one or more children may contribute, must in the aggregate suffice for this purpose. Here we are considering wages not from the standpoint of a 'labour policy' but from that of a tax policy.

But the issue of the labour 'costs' cannot be settled by confining our thought to the provision of physical continuity of labour. In a growing progressive community the crucial question is, "What is the minimum income any group of workers must receive in order to enable and induce them to continue their output of productive energy, and to provide such increase of labour-power as will increase that output, so as to meet the growing demands of a community increasing its numbers and enlarging its wants?" From the standpoint of practical economics this means, "What is the established and effective standard wage, below which a sufficiently large, skilled and reliable body of workers cannot be obtained?" The basis of such standard pay is in part the physiological considerations already touched upon, in part other conventional or 'moral' considerations, relating to standards of comfort which workers insist upon as conditions for the regular application of their labour-power. These standards and the relation of individual wages to them differ in various trades, in various parts of the country, and with the different opportunities for remunerative employment open to other members of the family besides the chief male wage-earner. But for our present purpose it is sufficient to recognize that the standard wage in any trade or locality is a necessary 'cost' of production, in that, if it is not paid, the requisite supply of labour is not forthcoming. It may perhaps occur to some that there remains a difference between the wage of physical subsistence, necessary to maintain the worker (and perhaps a family), and the supplementary portions which go to make up any standard wage containing elements of conventional expenditure and even including some elements of comfort or luxury, not always conducive but perhaps even detrimental to working efficiency. It may seem possible that such supplementary wage elements could be broken down under the pressure of wage competition, or could be encroached on by taxation, without affecting the supply of labour. And it must, I think, be admitted that there is some difference in the power of resisting taxation, or capitalist encroachment, between that portion of standard wage which rests on the firm rock of physiological necessity and that which does not. There have been periods in the industrial history of this and other countries when class standards of comfort have actually been broken down by the application of these outside economic forces. But for all that, we should be wise not to assign much value to such precedents in considering the actual economic situation of to-day. The conventional working-class standards of comfort in this country have been secured by a slow and on the whole continuous process of accretions during several generations, and they have recently been fortified by strong working-class sentiments of 'rights.' This moral support for class standards has further been reinforced by economic and political organization. Taking due account of such considerations, we should be justified in insisting that these standard wages (not merely the money they represent, but the purchasing power, the real wages) form an element in costs of production which is virtually irreducible. Nay, it is likely that in the post-war economic system the organized power of the workers will be applied effectively to achieve considerable advances upon the pre-war standards, enforcing them by the strike-weapon. It is sufficient here to recognize that standard wages, however composed and established, form a necessary 'cost' which has virtually no ability to bear taxation. A tax on low standards of wages would entail a loss of physical efficiency in the worker and his family, thus reducing the actual physical supply of labour power. A tax on the higher standards, reducing those elements of comfort or pleasure which figure most clearly in his consciousness, would be met by a 'moral' revolt of organized labour that would have the same injurious reaction upon industry. Standard wages are therefore necessary elements of income with no true power to bear a tax.

§ 2. It should be equally evident that in the existing economic system there is a minimum rate of interest, in payment for the production and use of capital, that must be secured to the owners of this capital to induce them to go on supplying it in the required quantities in this country to our industries. It may be that, under a purely socialistic system, if such could be established, no payment of income under the head of interest would be necessary: society would secrete the necessary capital in the ordered arrangements for its annual production. We are not, however, living in this society, but in one that depends almost wholly upon individual voluntary saving and application of savings under the prompting of personal gain. Such an economic system must secure to the individual saver and investor the payment that is absolutely necessary to induce him to save and invest. It would be foolish here to open up the familiar controversies about the nature and springs of saving and the moral justification of interest. It is unnecessary to do so, especially in a discussion confined to our national economy. It may be admitted that a good deal of saving would be effected in this country for the creation of capital, even if no positive interest were attainable. Even in poor and powerless societies many peasants and other people will 'save' for nothing, putting their savings in a 'stocking.' A large proportion of the saving of the rich classes in a developed industrial country is a virtually automatic process of laying aside for investment what is not wanted to support their conventional and personal standard of luxurious consumption. Most of it would go on, even if no interest were obtainable. The same is probably true of a part of the saving of the less well-to-do, who would continue to put aside money during their full earning period of life for their support in old age or infirmity, or even to assist their family after their death. Some of these people, it is rightly urged, would actually save more if interest were lower than it is, because it would be necessary to do so in order to secure a decent livelihood in their later years. But those who would draw from such admissions the conclusion that our national economic system would go on functioning, if no interest were attainable, are in double error. In the first place, there is a general agreement among economists that a considerable proportion of the national saving is evoked by the desire for interest, and varies directly with the rate obtainable. Just as some persons who love their work and would work for the love of it must be paid the common rate of wage or salary needed to evoke the energy of other workers in the same occupations who do not love their work and would withhold their energies if they were not paid, so with the saving classes, the willing savers must be paid at a rate determined by the insistence of the unwilling savers. Moreover, unless investment of savings in other countries is prohibited (a retrograde and injurious restriction upon freedom), the current world-rate of interest must be paid in this country for new capital. While, therefore, it is theoretically conceivable that, even in an economic system where the supply of new capital was left to individual saving, interest might fall to zero,[1] for the immediate future it is necessary to secure to the saving classes as a whole some positive payment, in order to induce them to withhold enough of their spending power from articles of immediate personal consumption in order to apply it to bringing new capital forms into being, and risking their loss in the processes of investment. In other words, just as there must be an immunity from taxation for a minimum standard wage, so there must be also for a minimum rate of interest upon invested capital.

§ 3. Profit is notoriously a slippery term, often overlapping and including elements of interest and rent. On any particular transaction it is generally taken as the difference between 'costs' and selling price. But, regarded as a form of income, it is the remuneration of the business man or entrepreneur for the work of organizing and conducting a business. This would include the planning of the business, the buying of the requisite materials, plant and labour, the direction of the productive power along certain channels, the marketing of the product, and the financing of the

---

[1] *I.e.* the motives which induce peasants to put money by 'in a stocking' 'for a rainy day' *might* suffice to provide the socially desirable amount of saving.

various operations. In some businesses, especially in the distributive trades, the success of the business turns so much upon the arts of buying and selling that the rate of profit depends mostly upon the difference between buying and selling prices. In joint stock enterprise, where nearly all the skilful critical acts of the entrepreneur are done by a salaried manager, only a portion of the profits goes in payment for these services; most of it passes into dividends, and is thus pooled with interest upon capital. But though difficult to pin for close definition, profit has a very real existence as a motive force in industry. If it be true that an intelligent and well-informed business man 'expects,' in putting his brains, energy, and capital, into a particular line of business, that he will make 10 per cent. upon his yearly turnover, any taxation which defeated that expectation would starve the trade of business ability and enterprise. This applies not only to the business man who institutes and 'runs' a business, but also to what we may call the expert or professional investors, as distinguished from those who merely put their savings in gilt-edged securities. It may be said that, though this consideration may reasonably set a limit to taxation falling on special sorts of business profits, any damage done to these trades would be compensated by others into which their ability and enterprise would be diverted, and that if all 'profits' were taxed indiscriminately, the business men would not allow their brains and enterprise to lie idle but would take what profits they could get. There is probably some truth in this view in the sense that existing business profits possess a large amount of elasticity. For profits, not wages, as some economists pretend, have been the 'residuary legatee' in the economic system, taking what remains of the product of industry, after the other factors have been paid their necessary hire. For it is the 'entrepreneur' in business who buys or hires at the market rate all the other instruments and materials, and who, after paying them their agreed price, keeps the remainder for himself. Even in a company with a salaried manager this is the case, though the profiteer is not always the shareholder. Often he is the group of financiers and directors who floated the company and took out the anticipated profits in advance in the terms of capitalization.

But the notion of some reformers that somehow or other the 'profits' of business can be eliminated as representing sheer waste or plunder in the present system is without foundation. Taking our system as it exists (and we are here not dealing with another system), it contains many types of business where what is termed a reasonable rate of profit must be secured to the men who organize and run them. Large settled businesses of a routine type can be run either as public services or under joint stock enterprise by salaried officials. But in new, changing and growing businesses the requisite initiative and energy will continue to need the personal incentive of speculative prizes. Fixed salaries will not secure these qualities. Moreover, business ability of a commanding type is more mobile and cosmopolitan than formerly, and were 'profits' too closely clipped in this country, would seek zones of freer exploitation.

These considerations, applied to profit, whether as speculative gains or as wages of management, need not imply that profits are in fact kept by effective competition at a minimum, and that any taxation placed upon them will starve or banish business ability. On the contrary, there is good reason to believe that the proportion of the total wealth distributed as 'profits' far exceeds the amount economically necessary to secure the application of the socially serviceable business ability. For not only is much of this profit predatory

or luck money, but the conditions of such effective
competition as applies to ordinary workers in
the trades or the professions often have no application in the higher business walks. When, therefore, the Income-Tax Reform of 1913-14 discloses
the fact that out of a total income of 1167 millions
coming under the survey of Somerset House not
less than 483 millions represented professional
and business earnings, we may take it for granted
that large excessive and fortuitous gains are included in this sum. If to these earnings under
Schedule D be added the financial profits and official salaries coming under Schedule B and E (both
of which will be much larger in post-war returns),
we shall recognize that profits, salaries, professional and official earnings undoubtedly contain a
large amount of economically unnecessary income,
or, in other words, income with ability to bear
taxation. To what extent this taxability applies
is a question to which we shall revert presently.
Here I am insisting on a recognition of the other
side, viz., the fact that all these incomes contain
substantial elements of necessary 'costs.' Profits,
salaries, professional earnings, in all the higher
grades, may possess large portions of income
which if taxed would not disappear, but a large

part of this income has the same immunity as other 'costs' of production.

§ 4. The net result of this analysis so far is to establish an all-important distinction between the sorts and sizes of income which rightly rank as 'costs' and those which are to be accounted 'surplus.' It is often said that we possess no means of discovering exactly where 'costs' end and 'surplus' begins, and that our distinction is a 'theoretical' one not suitable for fiscal application. This objection, of course, applies to all distinctions whatsoever, for in all classification there is debatable ground, one species shading off into another. For practical purposes this means the desirability of caution and for allowing a considerable margin of error. It does not mean that the distinction is for practical purposes invalid.

All taxing theory and practice have, in fact, been based upon some amount of discrimination between 'surplus' and 'costs,' though the discrimination has been loose and empirical. Every political financier has been largely occupied with finding sources of income which will not dry up under taxation, and in trying how far he can safely go in taxing them. Moreover, he is more or less cognizant of the sort of taxes which can be safely levied or increased without, as he would say, disturbing industry. Now elements of income which do not 'dry up' under taxation and the taxing of which does not disturb industry are precisely what we here call surplus-income.

§ 5. The classical political economy regarded what is termed economic rent of land as the type of surplus-income, and often confined the term to that income. According to Ricardo, rent was a natural surplus, consisting of the value of the produce of land in excess of the value of the produce of that land which just paid the necessary costs of cultivation. This theory assumed (1) that the worst land in use, *i.e.* at the 'margin of cultivation,' paid no rent, and consequently (2) that all economic rents were purely 'differential,' *i.e.* measuring the yield per acre over and above the marginal yield. These assumptions, however, as Adam Smith long before had recognized, are incorrect. The total supply of available land for any particular use, or even for all uses, may be so deficient that the worst land may yield a positive rent measuring the pressure of this scarcity of supply. In fact, there are many sorts and uses of land, and in such a country as ours, though the worst (marginal) land for rough grazing in some parts may pay a merely nominal rent, it is not true that the worst wheat-growing land does not pay a substantial rent, still less that the worst market-garden land in actual cultivation pays no rent. Each city has an actual or potential land supply of its own. The worst building sites have a high annual value, directly determined by their value for some alternative purpose such as market gardening or brick making. In a word, rents are not wholly differential: some of them are monopoly prices, measuring the power of the owners of a naturally scarce article to get a high price out of the needs of the public. Such rents taken by the worst building land, or wheat land, or other kinds of land, may be called specific or marginal rents.

These rents, whether marginal or differential, are pure surplus, and have what I here term an absolute ability to bear a tax. This unique nature of land, as he conceives it, is the basis of the contention of the Single-taxer. From the time of the 'physiocrats' it has been recognized that rent has no power to shift a tax imposed upon it. The popular mind has, however, no firm grasp of this truth, and persons who ought to know better often speak as if landlords had an unrestricted power to raise rents, so as to throw upon the tenants any increase of taxes and rates to which they are exposed. So far as the landowner is nothing but a landowner, this power does not exist. If rents

are sometimes raised 'on account of' rises in the
rates, it is usually because the properties have
previously been underrented, in the sense that the
landlord has not been extracting the utmost that
his position would have enabled him to get. The
rise of rates, threatening his net income, has led
him to look more closely to the economic power he
holds and to ask for and obtain a rise of rent
which he could, if he chose, have got before.

But there is another consideration. Most land-
values, whether agricultural or urban, do not
consist wholly of these economic rents. English
agricultural land has generally had more capital
put into it than would represent its selling value.
A good deal, often the whole, of the rent now
taken for it may be regarded as interest upon
past 'improvements.' This mixture of rent and
interest is, of course, most obvious in the ownership of town properties, and has an important
bearing upon taxability. Where the landlord is
the house-owner, he is not only a receiver of economic rent but of interest upon capital. In this
capacity he has some real power to raise his rent,
and so to shift a part at least of the new tax, or
higher rate, on to his tenant in the first instance.
For, if you tax not only the land value but the
buildings and other improvements, you lower the

net return on such investments and check the flow of new capital into building enterprises. Though the tax does not immediately reduce the supply of houses in relation to the demand, so that the landlord cannot at once shift any of the new tax or rate on to the rent, he will have the power to do so when the lease falls in, provided that the check upon new building makes a scarcity of houses. How much he can thus shift, and how quickly, depends upon the proportion which ground value bears to building value and the amount of competition there has been in the building business. Where there has been some sort of a monopoly in the development of a town or of a large estate in it, perhaps by the landlord's own enterprise or by a business arrangement with a contracting firm, the capital employed in the housing scheme will have been able to earn a rate of profit or interest considerably greater than would have been the case if building operations were open to the free competition of a number of rival contractors. In other words, some of the economic power of the site owner may be shared by the capitalists and entrepreneurs who helped to develop the estate.

This gives the key to the wider meaning of economic monopoly, or superior business opportunity, from which surplus elements of income are derived. Almost the whole of economic rents, both marginal and differential, could be taken in taxation without causing any reduction in the supply of land for any useful purpose. No owner would withdraw any of his land from its most remunerative use because of the high taxation to which the rent he drew was subjected, provided some fraction remained for him sufficient to induce him to put his land to its best use instead of allowing it to lie idle. A tax upon land value, assessed upon the most remunerative use to which the particular land could be applied, would itself be a strong incentive to compel the owner to put it to this use, for otherwise his residue of rent after he had paid the tax might be nil. Such a tax, therefore, instead of impairing the taxpayer's incentive to apply effectively his factor of production, would actually stimulate such application. Economic rent is a form of income upon which taxation could be put so as to absorb nearly the whole of it. The landowner would have no power to escape any taxation thus directly imposed, or shifted on to it from any source endowed with less ability to bear taxation.

§ 6. But this taxability is not, as single taxers have contended, a unique property of land values.

It is only because these values contain no element of 'cost,' consisting wholly of 'unearned,' or surplus income, that this highest degree of ability to bear attaches to them. Other incomes, in proportion as they carry the same element of surplus, also the result of 'monopoly' or superior economic opportunity, are similarly susceptible to taxation. I alluded just now to house property which, owing to restricted competition in building operations, was able to make a high return for the capital invested in it. The excess of this return over and above the ordinary market return for such an investment would be just as taxable, and just as unable to shift any of the tax, as would the land values of the sites on which the houses were built. If the capital thus advantageously invested were yielding a net 10 per cent. interest, as compared with the (say) net 6 per cent. which would suffice ordinary investors in such kinds of enterprise, the extra 4 per cent. would stand, as regards ability to bear a tax and inability to shift it, precisely on the same footing with the ground rent. This, of course, would not hold if the tax, instead of being confined to the surplus interest, were levied upon all income drawn from house investments, upon 6 per cent. investments as well as 10 per cent. investments. For in that case, as

I have already pointed out, the flow of fresh capital into building enterprise would be checked, a shortage of housing accommodation would ensue, and *all* house-owners would be able to raise their rents, including those who had been earning 10 per cent. In other words, this attempt to tax not surplus income only, but also some income which rightly ranked as costs, would enable the owners of surplus to shift the tax on to the tenants as well as the owners whose necessary 'costs of production' were assailed by the tax.

This extra 4 per cent. is not, as some economic writers describe it, quasi-rent, if by that be meant a feebler or merely temporary imitation of the economic rent of land. The use of the term quasi-rent is applied, by Professor Marshall and others, to the case of capital invested in buildings or any other fixed forms requiring considerable time for their production, which will have a temporary power to raise the price for their use, if a rapid increase in the effective demand for it takes place outstripping for the time all possibility of any corresponding increase of supply. Striking instances of such quasi-rents have been afforded by the experience of these years of war, in which sudden emergency-demands for building, machinery and other plant, have arisen under circum-

stances where the rate of fresh supplies of such
fixed capital not merely could not be accelerated
but often had to be reduced. Any existing plant
available or adaptable for producing munitions or
other war supplies has obviously been put for
the time being in an advantageous position as
regards its earning capacity; so far as bargaining
has not been subject to 'control.' The income due
to this advantageous position is called a 'quasi-
rent,' according to the accepted usage. I would,
however, deprecate altogether the shifty epithet
'quasi.' This temporary surplus income is a
short-time rent, as real as any of the more endur-
ing rents or extra-profits, and, what is relevant
to our purpose, just as able to bear a tax. In
ordinary times, however, such surplus gains are
generally of brief endurance. For though any
increased pressure of demand for buildings, plant,
etc., will give an immediate advantage to the owners of such forms of wealth, translatable into surplus income, this situation will immediately act
as a stimulus to direct more capital and labour
into these branches of production, so far as they
are free of access. This increase in the rate of
supply of plant, etc., will normally be rapid
enough to prevent the surplus income from rising
far or lasting long.

§ 7. The case from which we started differs, however, vitally from these instances of short business 'pulls,' or 'quasi-rents.' The advantage possessed by our owners of house-property, in an area of restricted competition, is based upon a monopoly or lasting scarcity as real as that of land itself. The high return upon such investment has no power to bring into the market an effective competition of new and equally well-placed houses. Upon the foundation of a natural scarcity has been created a scarcity value for this capital, as taxable as rent itself, though it ranks as profit on a business enterprise.

But this is only one instance of a surplus-income due to the possession of some economic coign of vantage, or some superior bargaining power, and associated with other elements of income which are genuine costs and untaxable. Close students of our actual economic structure are aware that the term competitive system is no longer applicable in any high degree to large departments of modern industry, commerce and finance. Everywhere in the more highly organized trades competition is giving place to combination. Were we to follow closely the various processes of production, transport and distribution, by which raw materials are grown, collected, carried, manufactured, and marketed as finished commodities, together with the supplementary processes which feed the main streams of production with machinery, tools, fuel and other subsidiary requisites, we should perceive innumerable places where the free currents were checked, impeded, and held up by powerful organized business groups able to take fixed toll upon the trade as it flowed through the straits where they had planted themselves, or which they had artificially created by the arts of combination. I need not labour the point. But it is to be insisted on that this interference with the free levelling force of competition, keeping prices down to 'costs' and incomes down to minimum requirements, cannot be disposed of under the slighting name of 'friction,' or treated as rare and abnormal. The business system of to-day is as much combinatory as competitive.

It is riddled with financial manipulation, trusts, cartels, pools, conferences, associations, and other arrangements by which businesses of distinct origin combine so as to control prices, and take profits higher than those attainable under free, or as they would call it, cut-throat competition. There is scarcely any large staple branch of manufacture in this country where strong 'combines' do not enjoy some such pull. The metal and textile trades, the important new industries of chemicals and electrical apparatus, furnishers to the building trades, the meat, milk and coal distributing trades, tobacco, cinemas and other luxuries, together with many necessaries such as cotton thread and wall papers, are 'controlled' in output, prices and profit, by some tight or loose form of combination, ranging from a complete amalgamation to a 'gentlemen's' agreement.

Such is the business world in which we are living, and after the war it will be 'more so.' For everybody is agreed that 'wasteful competition' must be got rid of wherever possible: the enforced combination during war conditions of hitherto competing firms will leave permanent effects. An active policy of Industrial Councils, primarily designed to secure more harmonious co-operation between capital and labour, must issue in closer relations between firms for the regulation of markets and prices. The maintenance of various government 'controls' for purposes of 'rationing' will make in the same direction of promoting organizations, which are quite unlikely to disintegrate when, if at all, the State removes its hands.

§ 8. This combinatory character of the new business world must challenge the new State to apply a fiscal policy directed to the conditions under which vast new surplus-incomes will emerge, derived from and proportionate to the new powers of combination. In certain instances the monopoly powers may be so pressing and pervasive, or in other words, the trades may be so fundamental, that the State policy will be one of complete nationalization. But it is unlikely that this process of direct State Socialism can go very far, or very fast, to cope with the new position we describe. The remedy which the State will apply to most cases of surplus-profits due to combination will be a taxation directed to divert large portions of these profits from private hands to the public treasury.

We have here the central problem of the new State finance, how to devise a taxing-system which shall secure as much as possible of these gains of combination without disturbing the energy and initiative of the business men who operate them, or diminishing unduly the flow of the new capital required for their enlargement and improvement.

Many of the surpluses will not be the product of some lucky chance or passing pull. They will flow from the ordinary structure and working of a trade, no longer subject to effective free competition. They will, no doubt, be limited in amount by some consideration of 'potential competition' if the surpluses are too exorbitant, as well as by considerations of the shrinkage of demand or recourse to substitutes where available. In other words, monopoly power is never absolute. On the other hand, within their limits the combinations exercise a lasting power to draw excess profits which have the same disability to resist or shift taxation as land itself. Very obstinate is the popular belief that, if you tax a manufacturer or tradesman, he can always take it out of you by raising his prices. But the belief is without foundation in fact. A monopolist or a combination, in control of selling prices, fixes them at the level which he calculates will yield him the maximum net profits on his business. Were he to fix this at a higher level, as he has the power to do, he calculates that he would be a present loser by cutting down demand, or a future loser by stimulating potential into actual outside competition. The fact that a portion of his extra-profits is taken in taxation will not enable him advantageously to raise his prices and throw the tax on the consumer.[1] High taxation may, of course,

[1] There are rare cases where the imposition of a tax might cause a monopolist to raise his selling prices, but there are as many where it might cause him to lower them. He has no normal power to raise them.

lead a combination to look more closely to its
control and to be more rigorous in its exactions
from the buyer. Or he may actually raise prices,
to his immediate loss, so as to rally public opinion
to demand a withdrawal of an unpopular tax.
But, apart from such tactics, there is no tendency
for a tax on surplus-profits to be shifted on to
the consumer. It will lie where it is put.

§ 9. The same capacity to bear a tax, and disability to shift it, apply to that part of earned
incomes sometimes termed 'rents of ability.' The
income of the ordinary working doctor or lawyer is, in ordinary times, considerably higher than
that of the ordinary artisan or clerk. It is sometimes supposed that this follows from, and is the
measure of, the higher qualities of skill involved
in his occupation. But there is no validity in the
assumption that pay varies directly and proportionately either with the skill or the social utility
of work. An agricultural labourer has much
more skill than a bricklayer, but his income is
much lower. A competent journalist is at least
as highly skilled as a leading K.C., but does not
earn a tithe as much. Neither what one may call
the standard rate, nor the individual rent of ability, is determined in the higher paid callings by

intrinsic skill or difficulty. To some extent the
higher standards of professional incomes may
rightly be accounted minimum interest upon capital expended in general and professional education and on the subsidies needed for these non-
productive years. If it is the case that a me-
chanic can attain his full earning capacity at
twenty, while an engineer or a doctor has to wait
till thirty, spending considerable sums on his keep
and training, the interest and sinking fund upon
this expenditure contained in the higher standard
of professional income does not figure as rent of
ability. It is a cost of production of the professional man, and as such is not capable of bearing
taxation. But, in so far as this capital expenditure is only within the reach of a small proportion of our youth, this restriction operates to keep
down the number of those entering the professions, and to enable them to organize and bargain
more effectively in marketing their services. To
some extent, no doubt, this tendency is affected
by the social prestige and intrinsic interests of
the professional life appealing to a very large
proportion of the middle and upper classes, and
causing some of the professions to be 'over-
stocked.' One or two professions, again, notoriously the bar, are so much loaded with subsidised

semi-amateurs that anything like a standard rate of income can hardly be said to exist. Moreover, almost all the professions have a considerable fringe of sweated labour. That is particularly true of the clerical, legal, medical and teaching professions. When, therefore, I speak of a standard professional income containing some element of rent or security-value that has a capacity to bear a tax, I must admit that such a standard-rate is far more difficult to discover than in any ordinary trade. And yet, I contend, it is right to assume that some such standard exists in each profession, though it may not be measurable. There is within reasonable limits a size of income which an ordinary professional man in fairly good position looks upon as sufficient and attainable in his particular calling. How much taxable capacity such a standard income possesses, having regard to the conflicting tendencies I have cited, will be matter of much disagreement. Perhaps these 'standard incomes' may rightly be deemed too 'theoretic' to be available for any taxing-system. But it is necessary to assume them, in order to deal with the individual 'rents of ability' which undoubtedly must rank as 'surpluses,' possessing some considerable capacity to bear taxation.

§ 10. What is true of the 'wages of ability,' as they are sometimes termed, in the business and professional classes, is also true of certain favourably placed classes of wage-earners. Though the great majority of wage-earners have no 'surplus' income in the sense here given to that term, there are in a good many trades certain skilled or important processes which are so strongly controlled by some organization of labour as to afford an income higher than accords with the grade of skill or strength involved, and higher than would be necessary to evoke a sufficient supply of competent labour for the kind of work. In the engineering and building trades, for example, there have generally been grades of men whose higher rate of pay has been recognized as due to closer organization and stronger power of bargain rather than to any intrinsic skill or knowledge. War experience has notoriously afforded many examples of this scarcity-power to exact a rate of pay containing an element of 'surplus.'

§ 11. I may summarize this analysis of 'ability to bear' in the following general terms. Those elements of income which are necessary payments to owners of productive agents, in order to sustain the productive efficiency of an agent and to evoke its application, rank as 'costs' of production, and have no ability to bear taxation. The standard wages required to keep a working-class family on such a level of efficiency and comfort as will maintain and evoke the regular application of its labour-power constitute labour 'costs.' Such salaries, fees and profits, as are necessary under existing and social economic conditions to secure the supply of the requisite amounts of business and professional ability needed for the initiation, organization and management of productive enterprise, must similarly rank as 'costs' of ability or brain-labour. To these must be added, under any system of private enterprise, the minimum interest required to evoke the amount of saving and the application of new capital needed to furnish the plant, tools and materials for the productive processes.

These 'costs' have properly no power to bear a tax. This does not mean, however, that taxation could not be imposed on them and might not lie there for a time. It means first, that if a tax were imposed on any of these 'costs' and did lie, the effort would be to reduce the volume of some productive power, either by lowering its physical efficiency, or by impairing the incentive for its owner to apply it as efficiently as it was applied before. Secondly, the reduction in the supply of

any sort of necessary productive power, thus
brought about, must cause such a rise in its price
(its wage, salary, profit or interest) as would
defeat the attempt to tax it, by enabling it to
shift the taxation on to those who bought
these productive services, or the products they
turned out. The elements of income which
are not 'costs' are 'surplus.' All economic rents
of land, whether 'scarcity' or differential rents,
all interest, profits, and other payments for
the use of capital, brains or labour, which are
due to superior economic opportunities and are
not necessary incentives to secure such use, will
rank as surplus. All forms of surplus have a
full ability to bear taxation. They have no ability to reject or shift it, and all taxes imposed by
a bad taxing policy or 'costs' tend to be shifted
on to some form or other of 'surplus.'

CHAPTER III

THE SHIFTING OF TAXES

§ 1. The distinction drawn between 'costs' and
'surplus,' and the principle of a taxing-policy
based upon it, will probably appear at first sight
too 'theoretic' for practical politicians. Granted

the general accuracy of the distinction, it will be urged, how are we to apply it in the complicated affairs of the actual business world? How are we to ascertain the sorts and the amounts of 'surplus,' and to disengage them for taxation from the 'costs' with which they are associated? Moreover, no State can 'scrap' its existing taxing-system and construct a brand-new one on these theoretic lines. We are deeply committed to certain taxes, whose productive value has a large body of experience to support them. We cannot throw them aside and take up new ones improvised in order to attach the various elements of 'surplus.'

Now I am well aware of the strength of certain portions of this criticism. I have no intention to propose the scrapping of our present taxing-system on the ground that it is not closely based upon 'ability to bear.' But I contend that it is useful, and indeed essential, to overhaul that system in the light of our taxing principle in order to remove bad taxes and so to reform our good taxes as to make them capable of absorbing as much of the 'surplus' as the needs of the new State require. If our identification of ability to bear taxation with surplus-income be admitted, it is possible to clear out of the way certain notions about taxation which are stumbling-blocks to reform.

The first of these is that every citizen who benefits by State expenditure ought to contribute from
his personal means to the upkeep of the State,
or that every class ought to bear its proper share
of the taxation. The chief defence of taxes upon
commodities of general consumption, as well as
of a 'universal income-tax,' proceeds from this
motive. To many it appears so obviously just
and socially desirable that its economic feasibility
is never questioned. But our analysis of Costs
and Surplus disposes of the notion by showing
that there are large classes of income which cannot bear a tax. The classes of the population
living entirely upon such incomes cannot contribute by taxation to the upkeep of the State. For,
if you tax this income, either directly or indirectly, you either reduce their economic efficiency
and productiveness and that of their family, or
you cause them to withhold some part of their
productiveness. If, for example, one accepts provisionally the minimum wage of family efficiency
estimated by Mr Rowntree at 44s. a week (reckoning post-war prices at 25 per cent. above pre-war
level), it is evident that any lowering of the income-tax limit to £100 per annum would defeat its
purpose by reducing the product of labour and the
total income of the community. This would be a

physically necessary result. Moreover, it is pretty certain that any reduction of the present war limit of £130, or the pre-war limit of £160, would be attended by the same economic damage. For it is not only the physiological minimum (44s.) that possesses this power to reject taxation. The worker will defend the current conventional standard of living, if it is assailed, by a refusal to do his full week's work.

The war lasted so long that for many classes of workers a higher standard of expenditure and of comfort won the support of habit and will offer a stiff resistance to taxation. Unless, therefore, there were a much greater drop of prices than is expected, it would be unsafe and impracticable to lower the income-tax limit, so as to make every citizen realize that he had to support the State. For the effect would be to cause a reduction in the output of efficient labour. Those who imagine that workmen would not take such action on account of what, after all, would be a relatively small demand upon their purse, are mistaken. Workers are extremely sensitive to such demands upon their narrow margin of superfluous income. There is abundant evidence that the lowering of limit to £130, and the more rigorous collection of the income-tax, have in fact been responsible for workmen 'playing' when a continuance of work would have brought their half-yearly income over the tax limit.

§ 2. A recognition of these difficulties often leads statesmen to resort to indirect taxation as a method of exacting some contribution from the wage-earners. The workers can, it is held, be made to pay in the capacity of consumers by means of taxes upon materials or commodities which are attended by a rise of prices. From the standpoint of short-range tactics and political expediency there is much to say in favour of this method. Most people prefer to pay their taxes in little fragments and without knowing they are paying. They resent any direct encroachment on their money income much more than a larger encroachment on their real income brought about by rising prices. The tariff-monger is well aware of this weakness. For even when he fails to convince his public that 'the foreigner will pay,' he knows that so many factors affect price that his profitable bit of protection can seldom be convicted as the sole cause of a considerable price-rise, and that most men do not follow price-changes with the same interest they give to wage-changes.

Hence the tendency to 'make the consumer pay.'

Now our analysis of 'ability to bear' makes it evident that in the last resort the consumer does not pay. Indeed, from the standpoint of real taxation there is no such person as the consumer. All taxation falls upon some element of income, and the consumer is not, as such, a recipient of income. It is so important to get this matter understood that I will take two illustrations.

First, let us take a tax on the money-wages of a class of workers whose earnings are just enough to maintain them and their families in economic efficiency. Suppose the employers were required to deduct a shilling from the weekly pay of such a class for income-tax. The loss of working efficiency thus caused means a reduction in the supply of this sort of labour-power without anything to indicate a corresponding reduction in the effective demand for it on the part of employers. Some workers will quit this sort of work now that their net money earnings are reduced; others will work less efficiently because their 'real' earnings have fallen: the flow of fresh young labour into this trade will slacken. The necessary result of a shortage in supply of labour-power thus brought about will be a rise in its price, i.e. competing employers will have to raise their wage-rate. This rise of wage-rate is in effect a shifting of the tax from the wage-earners—on to whom? The employer, in the first instance. The higher money wage he has to pay will raise his costs of production, and cut into his profits, unless he too can shift the tax on to some one else. Can he? The usual assumption, that he can, needs closer consideration. If he is a manufacturer or trader in such close competition with others that his profits only include a minimum interest on the capital employed (with allowance for risks), and the market price for his business ability, he has no more ability to bear this tax than the workers who shifted it on to him. If, on the other hand, his business is a member of a combine, controlling selling prices, or in possession of some other natural or acquired advantage which is represented in a rate of profit higher than the ordinary, the surplus profit thus indicated has the ability to bear this tax and will bear it. It will not pay this business man to put it on to the price of the articles he sells. For the possession of his surplus-profits implies that he has already exercised the power of a monopolist to fix selling prices above the limit of free competition, at a figure which will give him the largest quantity of surplus-profit. If it had paid him to fix a higher price than he had been charging, he would have done it. Now, therefore, that he is called upon to shoulder this tax he cannot shift it on to the buyer of his goods. It sticks upon his surplus-profit because this income has ability to pay.

The business men in a closely competitive trade, however, as we see, have no surplus-profit able to bear the tax. They will not merely be able, they will be compelled to put it on to the prices of the goods they sell, in order to make a 'living' profit, and to stay in the trade. So it seems to fall on 'the consumer.' Now our original workers who shifted the tax are themselves consumers, and will apparently as such be called upon to pay their share of the higher prices for the commodities they buy. But we started with the admission that their incomes had no ability to bear any of this tax, and this disability remains when the tax on their wages has by two shifts been brought back to them in the shape of higher prices. For their income which had no ability to bear was their real income, *i.e.* the goods they were able to buy with their money wage, and which they must buy in order to maintain their efficiency and that of their family. So, when this tax is put on again to them in the price of goods they buy, they will retain and exercise the original power to shift it. That is to say, they will de-

mand and get, by the pressure they brought to
bear in the first instance, another rise of wages
to enable them to pay these higher prices, thus
beginning once more the shifting process.

Here we may pause to ask whether other classes
of consumers, faced with this rise on prices, will
have the same power to shift the tax element the
prices contain. Our argument gives an affirma-
tive reply in those cases where the whole income
of the consumer consists of costs, *i.e.* minimum
payments for the use of his labour, ability, capital. No tax, direct or indirect, will lie on such
incomes of consumers. On the other hand, if consumers are in receipt of incomes containing surplus, they are not in a position to throw off the
tax by demanding a higher price for their factor of production. The tax will lie upon their
surplus income in the sense that, having the same
money income as before to meet the rise of prices
of commodities, they must buy less. This reduction in their 'real' income represents their ability to bear the tax. They hand over to the revenue some wealth which they would otherwise have
kept for themselves.

Thus we find no warrant for treating the 'consumer' as a person who can pay a tax. Consumers with 'surplus' income alone can pay, and

they pay out of this surplus. Consumers with no surplus incomes throw off the tax, which shifts until it finds some surplus elements of somebody else's income, the employer's monopoly profits, his landlord's rent, the royalties on some machinery, the elements in the income of well-to-do consumers that are in origin 'surplus.' On these elements the tax rests.

§ 3. If, instead of taking a tax on wages, we investigate a tax imposed upon some class of commodities, the same general line of reasoning applies. Here is a tax which appears to be directly levied on the consumer through a rise of price. But, in the first place, we have to note that it does not in all cases follow that a tax on commodities is actually attended by a corresponding rise of prices to consumers. If an *ad valorem* tax is collected from the manufacturer or merchant of an article, no doubt he will pass it on to the consumer, if he can. But whether he can depends upon whether he is in some degree a monopolist, or has exercised some power to 'regulate' prices above the competitive level. If he has, then he will not as a rule find it to his advantage to raise his prices further so as to make the consumer pay. The tax, in other words, would settle on his surplus. If, on the other hand, his prices have been determined by fairly effective competition, he and his trade competitors will have to raise their selling prices, and pass on the tax to the consumer. If, however, they were closely competing with foreign producers subject to no such taxation, they could not offer this resistance and would be taxed out of existence.

But in the incidence and shifting of taxes on commodities another distinction requires to be observed. On no two kinds of commodities would an *ad valorem* tax produce the same effect. Not merely is there some power to throw the tax on to the producer or trader, if his price contains a surplus element to bear it. But the actual rise in price where it is not thus prevented, will have two sets of effects, one upon consumers, the other on producers, which will be different in each case, and will affect the final incidence of the tax.

The effect on consumers will depend upon how important the particular commodity is upon which the tax is placed. Only in the case of what may be called an 'absolute necessary' *must* the tax be represented by a fully corresponding rise of price. A bread tax would presumably come nearest to an absolute necessary, and it would seem that a tax of, say, 3d. a loaf would enable the baker to put the tax on to the price. But even here there are qualifications. Unless all alternative foods were taxed in the same proportion, some other vegetable and animal foods would be in part substituted for bread. Moreover, it may be that, though some bread is absolutely necessary, there has been lax or excessive consumption among some classes of consumers which would be reduced by reason of the rise of price. If, owing to one or both of these causes, the attempt to put the 3d. on the loaf brought a reduction in the purchase of bread, the rise in price would settle somewhere below 3d., perhaps at 2d. The consumer (*i.e.* the producer with some surplus income) would bear the 2d. The other penny would be thrown back on to the miller and the farmer, and perhaps would ultimately settle on 'freight' or on the rent of wheat-land. Similarly with other taxes upon necessary commodities. The ultimate incidence of the tax will vary with the degree or intensity of the necessity, which in its turn will largely depend upon what untaxed alternatives are available. When we turn from necessaries to conveniences or comforts, everything again turns upon the strength of the hold which the particular commodity has upon the standard of comfort in the several classes of consumers. It is convenient to have a sound second suit of clothes, but it is not so necessary as to have a first suit. The high price of clothes has certainly stopped many people from purchasing a second suit to replace a worn-out one. It is comfortable to keep up a good fire, but the high price of coal, even before rationing, caused a marked reduction in domestic use. The strength of hold on a standard of consumption is a matter partly of material utility, partly of prestige. Many respectable persons will meet a rise of general prices, or a fall of income, by almost starving themselves at home, in order that they may maintain a reputable appearance in public. Conscious enjoyment is apt with many consumers to count heavier than material utility, when the absolutely physical necessaries are provided. Fine clothes and the cinemas have absorbed a large part of the recent rise in the wages of young women-workers. A rise in the price of such articles might have as its chief effort not a reduction in their demand, but a cutting down of other less obtrusive elements in the standard of consumption.

§ 4. But enough has been said to indicate the subtly psychological factors which here help to determine the effect of a rise of price upon demand for different classes of commodities. The incidence of a tax will vary with their subtle pressures. We can never treat any tax upon commodities as obviously transferable to the 'consumer,' even in the process of finding producers surpluses in which to settle. Some of it will generally pass, but how much no one can predict. Some of it will be thrown back on the various sets of producers or carriers or vendors. The way of doing this will often be a shrinkage in consumers' purchases, owing to an attempt to put the tax on to the price, which shrinkage will react upon the processes of production, reducing the use of the weaker or inferior land, plant, labour, and affecting both the normal costs of production and the 'surpluses.'

As an example of the intricate reactions of a tax, take the case of a new large tax on the sale of motor-cars and motor-cycles. Since these are mainly luxuries, the first recognized effect of any great rise of price that might follow would seem to be a great curtailment of demand. But such curtailment would check the rise of prices, fixing a new temporary price-level above the old one but not adding the whole of the tax. Some of the tax would thus be thrown on to producers for settlement where it can lie, for further shifting where it can not. Possibly a large part of such a tax might ultimately settle on mine-owners in Spain

or Sweden, or oil magnates in the United States
or Caucasus, or on tyre and other patentees whose
profits were soaring. But it is not certain that
a rise of price would be strongly resisted by consumers. In any period of great fluctuations of
trade where new men are 'getting rich quick,'
and where even young business men or well-placed
artisans are earning incomes far ahead of their
accepted standard of comfort, the personal prestige of possessing a motor-car or cycle might be
so powerful that the rise of price would prove a
feeble check on the rising demand. It would take
off a good deal of the money which would otherwise have gone either into other luxuries with less
prestige, or into the more substantial and older
elements of a standard of comfort, such as better
housing, or more expensive education of the children.

The case of such ordinary 'luxuries' as alcohol
and tobacco, strongly established in the standard
of comfort of most grades of the community, deserves a special consideration. In the case even
of the moderately well-to-do classes, it will be generally agreed that a substantial increase in price
due to taxation will be met, in part by a reduced
consumption (in quantity or quality of articles),
in part by an encroachment upon other elements

of unnecessary consumption, or of savings. The experience of war taxation, though abnormal in the sense that the natural economic reactions would be crossed or reinforced by 'patriotic' motives of economy, certainly produced these effects in the upper and middle classes. In a general readjustment of the standard of living for purposes of war economy, a smaller percentage of the year's expenditure would be given to those high-taxed luxuries. Such increased payments to the State (or the liquor and tobacco trades) as were actually made by these classes would come out of their surplus income, *i.e.* by reducing their expenditure on other luxuries or unnecessaries.

The more interesting problem arises in relation to working-class incomes, mostly containing nothing that can properly be regarded as surplus, in the sense that they do not exceed, and very often fall below, what is required for the proper maintenance of a family. Here it is evident that out of the higher money-incomes of the great bulk of the manual workers during the war, a considerably larger sum has been expended upon drink and tobacco, though probably a smaller percentage of their aggregate income. They thus appear to have paid, as consumers, a considerable quantity of these war taxes, though even here it

may be urged that their insistence upon satisfying strong-felt demands for higher priced liquor
and tobacco contributed towards the effective
pressure for higher money wages, so causing some
transfer of the tax on to their employers or other
owners of a 'surplus.'

But if this be so, what shall we say of the incidence of these taxes in ordinary times? Analysis of taxation shows that the working-classes, as
a whole, make their chief contribution towards
the public expenditure in the shape of payment of
these indirect taxes, and that the lower-paid
grades of workers pay in these ways a larger percentage of their total incomes in taxation than
do the better-to-do workers and the lower grades
of the middle classes. It is evident that in one
sense these taxes may be held to fall upon a 'surplus,' in another sense not. These taxed articles certainly represent an actual expenditure in
luxuries or comforts which constitute a surplus
element in expenditure, in the sense that an enforced reduction of such consumption would not
worsen and might improve the 'standard of living.' It is commonly argued that, if the workers can afford these kinds of expenditure, they
can afford to pay taxes, i.e. have some ability to
pay. And yet, on the other hand, this apparent

ability to pay is only due to a wasteful economy of actual income. Setting aside the question whether alcohol and tobacco are actually noxious, it is certain that working-class expenditure upon them carries an inability to pay for certain goods and luxuries needed for the health and efficiency of themselves and their families, *i.e.* represents a wasteful economy. There is no real surplus in these working-class incomes. This being so, any taxes they pay must normally be held either to encroach upon their truly necessary expenditure, or to be shifted on to some other incomes, *e.g.* those of their employers, through their insistence upon money wages high enough to support these 'luxuries.' There is, of course, the third alternative, that a tax may simply cause a corresponding reduction of expenditure upon the taxed articles. Only in the last case is it seriously defensible as a method of taxation. So far as the war taxes have brought about a reduction in the consumption of drink and tobacco that would have taken place had these taxes not been imposed, they are economically justified, not otherwise.

But while, in point of fact, the workers do contribute so large a percentage of their wages in these taxes, it is not open to anyone to urge that new taxes should be put upon them so that they may be made to pay 'their share' to the upkeep of the State. For if, in fact, the incidence of the existing taxes is upon the workers' income, they must be held already to be bearing a fair proportion of the taxes. On the other hand, if there is the power to shift such taxes, which I suspect, then it is a futile, and worse than futile, policy to set in operation a new and disturbing process of such shifting.

§ 5. But though every indirect tax will vary in its shifting and its incidence, according to the measure of free competition among producers and the amount of surplus-income among the various classes of consumers, these instances make it evident that in the last resort the tax tends to settle upon surplus elements of income which alone possess a true ability to pay. This doctrine may at first sight seem to make it a matter of indifference what sort of taxes are imposed, and who are called upon to pay them in the first instance. If all taxation, however imposed, settles upon the same surplus elements of income, why trouble to disturb the existing taxing-system, or why not defer to the weak preference which most people betray for secret forms of indirect taxation? Nay, does not such a doctrine play directly into the hands of protectionists, by its manifest implication that the surplus-incomes of foreign producers, merchants and exporters, can be made to bear a portion of the tariff duties we are urged to impose?

Believing, as we do, in the general superiority of direct over indirect taxation, it is of urgent importance here to state the grounds for this belief. The first is the waste and damage of the shifting process. In all economic movements there is a certain amount of inertia to be overcome. In the taxing process this means that the tendency to shift a tax that tries to settle upon 'costs' is met by another tendency for a tax to lie where it is put. If every tax laid upon income with no real ability to pay were shifted automatically and immediately on to the nearest surplus-income, fiscal convenience might often give preference to taxes on commodities which could be collected in large amounts from wholesale dealers. But such taxation always incurs the serious risks indicated in the very processes of shifting which we have described, some of it falls upon elements of necessary income.

Now the proof that such necessary income, *e.g.* a wage of efficiency, or a minimum profit, cannot bear the tax, is furnished in an actual shrinkage of the supply of labour or of capital in the affected trades. But this shrinkage is economically wasteful, and produces damage to the trade, which continues until the whole of the tax is actually shifted, and even later. Sometimes the shifting process is very slow, the tax lying long and causing a depression of the trade affected. In many countries oppressive taxation of the peasant class, or of town operatives, has permanently kept production to the lowest level of maintenance and stopped every incentive to industrial progress. Our contention, in other words, that a tax which cannot be borne without reducing the productivity of some class of producers will be shifted by inevitable economic forces, presumes a certain level of intelligent self-interest which does not everywhere exist. Accepted custom, for example, may prevent the operation of a tendency for wages to be raised in order to meet the raised prices due to taxation of foods or other necessaries, and as every standard of living has some elasticity, however slight, the standard may be lowered without the ultimate effects upon efficiency and productivity of labour becoming immediately apparent. Here is the chief danger of the insidious operation of most forms of indirect taxation.

Much harm is thus caused by what may be called the insensitiveness of the consumer in resisting taxation which he has no true or final ability to bear. This insensitiveness is due in part to ignorance, in part to slackness or indifference. It is this which gives a specious support to the prevailing notion that all increased taxation or rating put upon landlords is liable to be passed on to tenants in enhanced rent, and that traders can always put any fresh taxes on to the price of their goods. If tenants do not know what is the true rental value of their premises, they can easily be deluded into paying higher rents to compensate the landlord for a rise of rates, the delusion being accepted more readily because they shrink from the immediate inconvenience and cost of changing their residence. Similarly, a tax upon commodities or upon the materials which enter into them can often be made a source of actual gain, because the consumer, not knowing how much the tax adds to the costs of production, allows the tradesman to raise his prices far more than enough to cover the taxation.

§ 6. There are other dangers. It is of urgent importance in the practice of popular self-government that the fixed system by which a State raises and expends revenues shall be open and intelligible to its citizens. The actual incidence of taxation ought to be known to all. The notion that

any sound political end is served by making
everybody appear to contribute to the State revenue, irrespective of the fact that many persons
have no ability to pay, is mere feeble-mindedness.
Such concealment of the facts of the case can
only help to obfuscate the civic intelligence. Nor
is it less important that the political directors of
fiscal policy shall learn from sound experience
what are the income-elements capable of bearing
taxation, so that all increased demands for revenue may be met by equitable and innocuous methods.

So far I have applied myself to showing:

1. That all taxes must be treated as deductions
   from real income.
2. That income is divisible into (a) economically
   necessary payments for the use of factors
   of production, i.e. costs; and (b) unnecessary or excessive payments, i.e. surplus.
3. That all taxation should be directly laid upon
   surplus, because if any taxation is put on
   'costs,' the process of shifting it on to
   'surplus,' first, involves waste and damage to production and is frequently made
   a source of extortion from consumers;

secondly, deceives the public by conceal-
ing the final incidence.

§ 7. Before winning acceptance for this treatment as a basis for reformed taxation in the new
State, it will, however, be necessary to meet several lines of criticisms, partly directed against
the 'economics,' partly against the practical politics of any wholesale application of the theory.

The first objection will take this shape: "Your
treatment of 'costs' is entirely directed to a static
condition of industry and commerce, to the mere
maintenance of existing instruments of production. You appear to assign the whole of your
surplus (consisting of rent, surplus-interest,
profits, salaries, etc.) as a body of income possessing an unlimited ability to pay. But you for-
get that from this fund is derived the saving
which forms the fresh capital required for industrial and commercial progress. If you are prepared to hand over to the State all this surplus,
you will make economic progress impossible."
This objection imputes an undue stress upon the
origins of surplus, as distinct from the uses to
which such surplus will or may be put. Even the
economic rent of land, it will be urged, does not
possess unlimited ability to pay, if we bear in mind

that a tax approaching 100 per cent. would diminish national savings by the proportion of such 'unearned' income as would have been saved and applied to capital had it been left in the landlords' hands. As for 'surplus' income from businesses, the bulk of the new capital required for the enlargement and improvement of plant, materials and processes, to say nothing of increased employment of labour, comes from this source. This criticism has been vigorously directed against the excess-profits taxation of wartime, which has removed large sums that might have been 'put back' into the business, or been employed in starting new enterprises to meet post-war demands.

§ 8. Now, in part, this criticism has been anticipated and met by my definition of costs. For in distinguishing costs from surplus in industry, I included under 'costs' not only such a minimum interest and profit as were needed to maintain existing plant and business ability, but such as would evoke an increasing supply of these factors so as to provide for a progressive industry. How far this places a limit upon taxation of rents, profits, interest, depends, however, to a considerable degree upon the post-war structure of industry and the uses made by the State of the public income raised out of private surplus.

If, as may confidently be assumed, a large part of that body of industry, hitherto in private hands, which has passed out of the competitive era into the era of combination, now passes into State or municipal enterprise, the surplus-income it yielded to its private owners should be available for the public, unless in some instances the public authority yields the potential surplus to the public in the shape of lower prices. If railways, mines, electric supply, banks and insurance businesses, the drink trade, large sections of the housing and distributive trades, became public businesses, private saving will no longer be needed to feed their enterprises with new capital: that provision will henceforth be made by the State and the Municipality. Bearing in mind that the type of industry thus socialized will comprise most of the greatest capitalistic enterprises, it will appear that the defence of surplus against taxation because of the need of making provision for the improvement fund is considerably weakened. The State will make the necessary savings for nationalized industries out of the income of those industries. There will, in respect of these businesses, be no failure to provide the needed income

of capital. As for the surplus-producing industries which it may be convenient to leave in private hands, it by no means follows that the taxation of their surplus will imply a reduction in the
aggregate of new capital available for national industry. The new State is pledged to many operations, such as housing, land development, afforestation, education, in which considerable capital expenditure will be involved. To divert
surplus-income which might, if left in private
hands, have furnished an increase of private industrial capital, into these productive State em-
ployments, involves no net reduction in capital or
employment of labour.

But even if the taxation of surplus-income did
imply a reduction in the rate at which new industrial capital, private or public, was created, this
is no condemnation of the policy. Labour and
ability are even more important factors of production than capital, and any improvement in
their efficiency may be cheaply purchased by some
diminution in the growth of industrial capital.
Public expenditure on health and education, in
particular, will, wisely directed, add immensely to
the future productivity of the nation. For capital is, after all, only the servant of productive
ideas. The cultivation of the mind of the nation

for the creation, selection and application of new productive ideas is the most profitable of all uses of revenue. Hitherto too much of the national surplus has been put into increasing the capital structure, too little into improving the physical and intellectual calibre of the people.

Though industrial development is by no means the final test and justification of taxation, an enlarged public revenue, well applied to general purposes of national welfare, will assuredly carry a great enlargement of the productive forces of the nation. An intelligent administration of public services will make a more socially advantageous use of surplus-revenue than would be made by private business men capitalizing it for their own profit.

§ 9. The conception of a national industrial system, with privately owned capital as its foundation and profit as its regulative motive, has long been exposed as an insecure basis for social order. The economic surplus, the fund for social progress, must pass more and more under the direct administration of Society. In order, however, that the justice and utility of the proposal be rightly grasped, the origin and nature of the fund that constitutes this surplus should be comprehended. The notion that taxation is *prima facie* an encroachment by an outsider, the State,

upon the rightful property of individual citizens,
only justified by necessity of State, is still widely
prevalent. Its falsity is implied in the analysis
which I have brought to bear in these chapters,
wherein surplus is shown to arise as the result of
some economic inequality or monopoly power
wielded by the person who receives the surplus.
But there is another way of looking at the same
phenomenon which makes an even stronger case
for Society as the rightful recipient of the surplus.
It is not enough to represent these rents, excessive profits and other elements of surplus, as not
earned or created by the persons who receive
them as income. They are directly produced by
the operation of social needs, institutions, and
activities. An individual acting by himself can
create no wealth. The materials and tools with
which he works are supplied to him by elaborate
processes of social co-operation. The skill he applies to their use has been laboriously acquired
by past generations of men and communicated to
him by education and training. A highly com-
plex division of labour, based upon co-operation
in the industry and workshop, prescribes and
gives 'value' to his particular job. The market
which finally stamps what is called his product
with utility, as capable of satisfying some

human want, is itself a highly social structure. Finally, the organized community, as a State, protects and assists both the individual producer and the various social institutions and processes which help him to produce. Thus Society co-operates everywhere with the individual producer and assigns to the product its 'value.'

Though the State is only the political organ of Society, it is the protector and support of all the other forms of social organization, and is often the regulator and director of the economic forces of Society by means of legal and administrative action. The whole of the functions of the modern State subserve the processes of production of wealth, though it has other more important human ends. When the State directly undertakes an industry, such as letter-carrying, it can defray its expenses out of retail prices charged to its customers. The new State may, in taking over other fundamental industries, such as railways and mines, similarly draw revenue from these specific undertakings. If it chooses, and the nature of the industries allows, it may take a profit from such undertakings which it may apply to pay the expenses of other public services not of a directly remunerative character, such as justice, defence, education and public health. But for the bulk of its revenue it must rely upon taxation of incomes and properties derived from privately owned undertakings. It is, therefore, important to recognize that its claim to this taxable income is not confined to the general plea of public necessity, but is also based upon the express part taken by the State in assisting to create the economic product and to give it value.

The State, thus regarded, is a rightful participant on its own account, in every product whose whole value is, in the first instance, for convenience distributed as private income, and has a claim for its share upon the several recipients. What is that share? No theoretically exact answer, I think, can be given to this question, so intricate is the co-operation between individual and social energies and needs in modern economic operations. But I suggest that a reasonably sound apportionment of claims would leave to the individual his full personal costs of maintenance and growth, *i.e.* such income as suffices to support in full current efficiency himself and his family and to evoke such increased efficiency as they are capable of, while assigning to the State, as the organ of a hitherto under-nourished Society, any surplus-income which chance, combination or other natural or contrived conditions, may enable a business to obtain. This may not be an absolutely scientific principle of distribution. But, in view of the presumption hitherto prevailing, viz., that the whole of the product was the rightful property of those to whom it passed as private income, and that the State's share should be kept at a minimum, the principle here proposed, by which the State becomes the residuary legatee after all expenses of upkeep and of reasonable growth are provided out of income, should be acceptable to those who realize the growing needs of the new State.

§ 10. I have already anticipated, in part, the claim that reasonable 'expenses of growth' should include some adequate provision of increased capital in a business capable of useful expansion, and that the portion of excess or surplus profits needed for application to this object should not be taken in taxation. So long as saving and investment remain private functions, this seems a reasonable claim. For though, as I have contended, the diversion of such savings from private possessors to the purposes of State does not necessarily imply a less productive use, there is a *prima facie* case in favour of furnishing an adequate supply of new capital for healthily growing private enterprises. This need could be met in one or two ways. The Income-Tax Commissioners could be instructed to make allowances or exemptions in respect of such portions of the income of a business as was 'put back' into the business. If the necessary supervision and accountancy took place, this might be a sound social policy, for the State would later on reap its gain in the taxation of the larger income issuing from the enlarged business and from the inheritance duties when the untaxed capital passed at death. The alternative method, a discussion of which lies beyond the scope of this inquiry, consists in the State itself supplying, through its own National Bank or other loan system, the new capital required by businesses which still remain under private management; in other words, the substitution of public saving and investment for private, a process of gradual nationalization applicable to the whole or any part of growing private enterprise.

For immediate purposes, however, we may dismiss this method of public finance and give a provisional acceptance of the allowance system, with such safeguards as would be needed against certain obvious abuses. During the next few years, at any rate, it may be serviceable that our taxing-system should guarantee inducements, in the shape of tax exemption, to the allocation of large shares of business earnings to the capital fund, so as to make good the letting down of some important kinds of plant and the failure during the war period to make normal provision for improvements.

But all such exemptions should be limited in amount and confined to the case of vital industries, and a thorough scrutiny into the merits of each application should be undertaken by the Income-Tax Commissioners. Such a provision need not be held to invalidate the application of our general principle that the State is the residual owner of all income which exceeds the requirements of maintenance and normal growth.

This identification of the surplus with the income that expresses the aid rendered by the State, as the representative of Society, to the production of wealth, gives, I venture to suggest, a new moral as well as economic basis for the finance of the new State.

CHAPTER IV

THE TAXATION OF INCOME

§ 1. Accepting as the test and measure of 'ability to pay' the distinction between costs of production and surplus-income, it may at first sight

be obvious that a sound and equitable taxing-
policy will levy taxes directly and exclusively
upon those economic rents, high dividends and
profits, swollen salaries and professional earnings, which comprise this surplus. A large school
of single-taxers has always demanded that the
whole of the tax-revenue should be raised by taxing land values, or their annual yield, up to 20s.
in the £. Economic rent is, they affirm, the income furnished by Nature for the support of the
social institution called the State. It is, they
maintain, the only fund which can be attached
without robbing some one of his rightful earnings,
or diminishing some useful incentive to production. The landowner alone has a true ability to
pay.

Now, setting aside the fact that the highest possible estimate of the annual land value of this
country could not furnish more than a quarter of
the revenue required for the post-war State, there
is a further objection to the single-tax which in-
validates for practical purposes the whole policy
of attaching by taxation the separate elements of
surplus that emerge in the operations of business.
Though separable from capital for purposes of
economic analysis, land-values are so blended with
improvements and with other forms of capital, for

all practical operations both of industry and finance, that a rigorous separation for taxing-policy is neither feasible nor equitable. The actuarial difficulties have been illustrated in the clumsy, expensive, and unsatisfactory endeavours to measure land-values and their increments under the provisions of the 1909 Budget. But when a fuller analysis of industry discloses the innumerable ways and degrees in which elements of land-value are embedded in all parts of our economic system, the difficulty of any reliable measurement is found insuperable.

These technical difficulties, however, are not the chief ground for rejecting such a proposal. Modern operations of capitalization, purchase and investment, have so closely identified land-values with capital, and the identification has been so strongly endorsed by law and custom, that their separation now for taxing-policy would involve intolerable injustice. A has invested £1000 in a Trust Company which, quite unknown to A, puts the funds into land or mines. B invests £1000 in another Trust Company which puts its funds into industrials or foreign rails. Under a single-tax A would lose everything, B nothing, though both were actuated by precisely the same motives and performed acts of saving and investment which to them were indistinguishable. During the last two years hundreds of large estates have been broken up and sold by their owners to their tenants. Clap on a single-tax after the war, and these purchasers lose all their savings, while the former owner goes off with his untaxed gains.

§ 2. The iniquity of such a taxing-policy is too glaring to need lengthy exposition. I cite it chiefly as an entry into a more pertinent criticism applicable to the whole attempt to discriminate detailed items of 'surplus' for taxing purposes. At first sight it is plausible to suggest that, in order to get for revenue as large a share as possible of the monopoly or surplus profits of combinations or well-placed business companies, the whole or the bulk of the net profits over and above the sum needed to pay the minimum dividends required to maintain the capital should be taken by taxation. Here is a strongly established combination earning a regular 20 per cent. profit, why not take for the State the bulk of the profit that represents mere surplus, by means of a tax graduated steeply, not according to the aggregate net income of the business, but according to the dividend? A sufficient motive to operate the business in the most efficient and productive manner might be provided under a taxing-policy which would get four-fifths of the excess profits for the revenue.

But the same difficulty presents itself as in the case of land-values. If the whole of the share-capital of such a business as we are considering were held by the original promoters and investors, the project would be feasible and equitable. But where, as in most such cases, a very large proportion of the shares have changed hands in the operations of the stock-market, there is no presumption that the present shareholders are receiving upon their investment a dividend which contains any surplus. The surplus, present and prospective, has been taken out of the concern by the original shareholders, or by interim shareholders from whom the present holders have bought their shares at market prices enhanced by the excessive earning power of the Company. A pays £1000 for four £100 shares in a profitable combine whose shares stand at a premium of £150 per share. B pays £1000 for ten £100 shares in an ordinary competitive business, where the shares stand at par. A and B get the same actual amount of annual dividend for their respective investments. But the suggested taxation which would take the 'surplus' earned by A's Company would reduce his earnings on each £100 he invested to, say, 1 per cent., while B would be receiving his full 5 per cent. on his £100. This discrimination would be obviously unjust. In other words, when, as is common, the future 'surplus' has already been secured by a shareholder who has sold out, it is impracticable to get that surplus for the revenue by a tax imposed upon the income of the purchaser of the shares. As in the instance of the landowner who has scooped in the whole rise of land-values by the terms of his sale, so here, if the tax-gatherer is after the 'surplus,' he must seek it where it lies, viz., in the possession of the vendor of the shares.

There are two ways in which this can be done, either by a reform of the assessment for income-tax, which brings into the assessible income for the year the net gain obtained by such a sail of shares, or by leaving the gain with other gains to accumulate during the lifetime of the recipient for taxation when his estate passes at his death. The relative value of these two methods may be discussed later. At present it suffices to register a clear judgment to the effect that it is not feasible or equitable to attempt to earmark and attack for revenue the separate items of surplus as they emerge in the present distribution of rent or dividends or profits.

The upshot of this investigation is to indicate a general income-tax as the most serviceable instrument for securing to the revenue a large share of unearned income or 'surplus.' The fact that during the last half-century this tax has passed into the permanent finance of the country and has occupied a place of ever-increasing importance, is itself a strong recommendation. For new taxes are not merely unpopular: they are usually precarious both in incidence and yield, having no body of financial experience to support the calculations of the taxing authority.

§ 3. It is, therefore, to the general income-tax that we should look as the first means of enabling the State to get its revenue out of the surplus-elements of income possessing ability to pay. And it must operate, not by attempting elaborate discrimination of the origins of income, but by attention, in the first place, to its size; in the second, to the number of persons dependent upon the income for their maintenance and efficiency.

Now, having regard to our analysis of the economic nature of income, it should not be difficult to gain assent to the proposition that 'surplus' and its presumed 'ability to pay' vary directly with the size of income. There is a presumption that a large income contains a large amount of 'surplus,' in the sense of payments not needed economically to evoke any productive energy on the part of the recipient, and that a small income contains none of this surplus.

But this presumption is crossed by another, relating to the consumptive utility of the income. We have agreed that the part of any income needed for the maintenance and improvement of a worker and his family ranks as 'costs' and not as 'surplus.' It is clear, therefore, that the quantity of taxable surplus in the family income varies with the size and needs of the family. An income of £500 a year may have a not inconsiderable surplus, if it has only one man or woman to maintain. But if it has a man, his wife, and six children to maintain there may be no surplus.

If, then, we are to adopt as our main instrument of taxation a general income-tax, based on the presumption that surplus varies with income, an allowance must evidently be made for this qualifying circumstance. The early recognition of this equitable principle by the allowances in respect of dependents in our income-tax, is quite inadequate. For it is impossible to contend that an allowance of £25 represents anything approaching a true maintenance, in respect of families with an income not exceeding £500. Properly applied, the principle must be based upon the assumption that the cost of maintenance of every human being is the same. For though this may not be strictly true, it is the only practicable method of procedure. It is, therefore, desirable that this equality of maintenance principle shall be applied to the full extent for all incomes of a low or moderate order. The true policy is thus stated by Mr Sidney Webb:[1] "What is suggested is that, so far as incomes not exceeding £2500 a year are concerned, whether earned or unearned, it should be open to any person assessed to ask all that the taxable receipts of all the members of his family, living in the same household with him and sharing in its expenses, or maintained elsewhere wholly or partially at his expense, should be aggregated for assessment as a Family Income; and that Family Incomes so arrived at, should, for income-tax purposes, be divided by the number of members of the family (husband, wife, children, step-children, father and mother or grandparents only) *actually maintained therefrom*. There could then be allowed from the combined Family Income, in respect of the persons maintained therefrom, whatever Abatement each portion of such income would justify, if it were that of one person only."

[1] "How to Pay for the War," p. 237. (Allen & Unwin).

"The result would be that a bachelor or spinster,
living independently, and apart from his or her
near relations, would normally pay income-tax as
at present. A married couple without children
might apply to have their combined aggregate of
incomes divided by two, and if this brought these
halves below £700 each, they would be entitled
to two of the Abatements allowed on such incomes.
The father of a family of four children might apply in the same way, aggregating all the incomes
of himself, his wife and his children, and divid-
ing the sum by six. This might bring him six
Abatements instead of one (or possibly none).
In the extreme case a Family Income of £2500
might conceivably be allowed as many as sixteen
Abatements, if as many as sixteen members of
the family were being maintained therefrom—
in exactly the same way, in fact, as if the incomes
were legally divided among all these separate
members of the family, and they had to make separate returns for taxation." Whether the limit
of £2500 here suggested may not be unduly high,
is an open question, the answer to which will presumably depend upon the post-war level of prices
and the standard of expenditure needed for the
efficient maintenance of an individual. But the
policy is equitable and economically sound. Its

essence lies in securing that taxation shall not be imposed upon the expenses of maintaining human efficiency, or, in other words, upon 'costs.' It is not a new principle of taxation, but an adjustment of our accepted principle of ability to pay to the circumstances of the family as the unit of expenditure.

§ 4. Admitting this important provision for taking into account the number of dependents in the application of a progressive income-tax to the lower and medium incomes, the rule that rising incomes imply a presumption of increasing surplus and a corresponding increase of ability to pay, may be accepted as valid. It is already in force by the united policy of allowances, abatements and super-tax, crossed by the distinction between earned and unearned income. Now I suggest that all these special arrangements and discriminations are clumsy and wasteful, that they should be swept away and replaced by a single progressive curve of valuation, according to which every taxed income would pay a different rate of taxation according to its size.

The defective progression of the present tax is well illustrated in the following Tables from the last available Report of the Inland Revenue Commissioners (1918). Though changes made in last year's Budget effect certain minor changes in graduation, accompanied by considerable changes in rate and sums payable, the Tables still hold good for the purpose of illustrating defects of graduation.

Although a continuous graduation is here carried up to the limit of £3000, where the super-tax then comes in, this graduation shows two sorts of grave deficit. First, the sudden jumps in tax-rate per £ and in amounts payable at certain arbitrary points in the rise of taxable income. These occur at eight points, viz., £401, £501, £601, £701, £1001, £1501, £2001, £2501. In each case an increase of £1 in taxable income makes a sudden addition to the rate and amount payable. On the higher levels of income the sudden addition of £1 to the amount payable may not arouse much feeling of grievance, but in the lower levels it is distinctly felt and operates injuriously in keeping down declared incomes. Again, it is just upon the lower levels of income that the sudden leaps in the rate of taxation are greatest. At £401 there is a sudden rise of ½d. in the £ on the income or earned income, whereas two jumps at £1001, £2001, respectively, are only ⅓d., and at £2001 only $\frac{1}{10}$d. in the £. This slackening of the pace

TABLE 9.—Showing the Actual Amount and Effective Rate of Income-Tax payable for each of the years 1916-17 and 1917-18 in the case of certain Incomes taken as examples.

Income (1)	Abatement (2)	Net Income taxed. (Col. 1 less Col. 2) (3)	Where the Income is wholly Earned — Rate of Tax on Income in Col. 3 (4)	Amount of Tax Payable (5)	Effective Rate on each £1 of Income in Col. 1 (6)	Where the Income is wholly Unearned — Rate of Tax on Income in Col. 3 (7)	Amount of Tax Payable (8)	Effective Rate on each £1 of Income in Col. 1 (9)	Where the Income (Col. 1) is mixed and assuming that half is Earned and half Unearned — Amount of the Income in Col. 3 which pays Tax At the Rate in Col. 4 (10)	At the Rate in Col. 7 (11)	Amount of Tax Payable (12)	Effective Rate on each £1 of Income in Col. 1 (13)
£		£	s. d.	£ s. d.	d.	s. d.	£ s. d.	d.	£	£	£ s. d.	d.
131	120	11	2 3	1 4 9	1.8	3 0	1 13 0	1.8	—	11	1 0 0	1.8
150	120	30	2 3	3 7 6	5.4	3 0	4 10 0	7.2	—	30	4 10 0	7.2
200	120	80	2 3	9 0 0	10.8	3 0	12 0 0	14.4	—	80	12 0 0	14.4
250	120	130	2 3	14 12 6	14.0	3 0	19 10 0	18.7	5	125	19 6 0	18.5
300	120	180	2 3	20 5 0	16.2	3 0	27 0 0	21.6	30	150	25 17 0	20.7
350	120	230	2 3	25 17 6	17.7	3 0	34 10 0	23.7	55	175	32 8 0	22.2
400	120	280	2 3	31 10 0	18.9	3 0	42 0 0	25.2	80	200	39 0 0	23.4
401	100	301	2 3	33 17 3	19.5	3 0	45 3 0	25.7	101	200	40 0 0	23.9
450	100	350	2 3	39 7 6	21.0	3 0	52 10 0	28.0	125	225	47 16 0	25.5
500	100	400	2 3	45 0 0	21.6	3 0	60 0 0	28.8	150	250	55 7 0	26.5
501	100	401	2 6	50 2 6	24.0	3 6	70 3 6	33.6	151	250	64 0 0	30.5
550	100	450	2 6	56 5 0	24.5	3 6	78 15 0	34.4	175	275	70 0 0	31.0
600	100	500	2 6	62 10 0	25.0	3 6	87 10 0	35.0	200	300	77 10 0	31.3
601	70	531	2 6	66 7 6	26.5	3 6	92 18 6	35.3	231	300	78 10 0	32.8
650	70	580	2 6	72 10 0	26.8	3 6	101 10 0	37.6	255	325	88 15 0	33.3
700	70	630	2 6	78 15 0	27.0	3 6	110 5 0	37.8	280	350	96 5 0	36.0
701	—	701	2 6	87 12 6	30.0	3 6	122 13 6	42.0	351	350	97 0 0	36.0
800	—	800	2 6	100 0 0	30.0	3 6	140 0 0	42.0	400	400	120 0 0	36.0
900	—	900	2 6	112 10 0	30.0	3 6	157 10 0	42.0	450	450	135 0 0	36.2
1000	—	1000	2 6	125 0 0	30.0	3 6	175 0 0	42.0	500	500	150 0 0	42.0
1001	—	1001	2 6	125 2 6	30.0	3 6	175 3 6	42.2	501	500	151 0 0	42.1
1500	—	1500	3 0	225 0 0	36.0	4 0	300 0 0	48.0	750	750	252 10 0	49.0
1501	—	1501	3 0	225 3 0	36.0	4 0	300 4 0	48.1	751	750	283 10 0	49.1
2000	—	2000	3 8	366 13 4	44.0	4 6	450 0 0	54.0	1000	1000	408 0 0	58.1
2001	—	2001	3 8	366 17 0	44.1	4 6	450 4 6	54.1	1001	1000	409 6 0	58.1
2500	—	2500	4 4	541 13 4	52.0	5 0	625 0 0	60.0	1250	1250	583 6 0	58.1
2501	—	2501	4 4	541 17 8	52.1	5 0	625 5 0	60.0	1251	1250	584 6 0	58.1
3000	—	3000	5 0	750 0 0	60.0	5 0	750 0 0	60.0	1500	1500	750 0 0	60.0

of progression is a palpable defect, discernible both in the earned and the unearned columns.

Table 17 in the same Report, carrying up the matter into the range of the operation of the super-tax, exhibits the same defects, a large slowing down in the rate of progression in the higher incomes. Though the tax rates and the amounts payable have both been raised since this Table was constructed, the criticism still holds good.

TABLE 17.—Showing the actual amounts of Income-Tax and Super-Tax payable for each of the years 1916-17 and 1917-18 in the case of certain incomes taken as examples, and the effective rate of the combined taxes.

AMOUNTS OF TAX.

Income.	Income-Tax.			Super-Tax.			Income-Tax & Super-Tax.			Effective Rate on each £1 of Income.
£	£	s.	d.	£	s.	d.	£	s.	d.	d.
3,025	756	5	0	22	5	10	778	10	10	61.8
4,000	1,000	0	0	79	3	4	1,078	3	4	64.7
5,000	1,250	0	0	154	3	4	1,404	3	4	67.4
6,000	1,500	0	0	245	16	8	1,745	16	8	69.8
7,000	1,750	0	0	354	3	4	2,104	3	4	72.1
8,000	2,000	0	0	479	3	4	2,479	3	4	74.4
9,000	2,250	0	0	620	16	8	2,870	16	8	76.6
10,000	2,500	0	0	779	3	4	3,279	3	4	78.7
20,000	5,000	0	0	2,529	3	4	7,529	3	4	90.3
30,000	7,500	0	0	4,279	3	4	11,779	3	4	94.2
40,000	10,000	0	0	6,029	3	4	16,029	3	4	96.2
50,000	12,500	0	0	7,779	3	4	20,279	3	4	97.3
75,000	18,750	0	0	12,154	3	4	30,904	3	4	98.9
100,000	25,000	0	0	16,529	3	4	41,529	3	4	99.7

Now there are various methods by which these defects of the sudden jump and the degressive rate of advance in higher income can be remedied.

The most practical which I have seen is that proposed by Mr J. Zorn in the following Tables. His method of progression is by a process in which the rise of rate of tax in the £ accumulates pace as it proceeds, by means of a four-speed gear. The first speed operates from incomes up to £500 by a rise of 3d. in the £ for each successive £100. The second operates from incomes from £600 to £1000, by a rise of 6d. in the £ for each successive £100. The third proceeds by rises of 1s. in the £ on each £1000 from £1000 to £10,000. The fourth takes a rise of 1s. 6d. in the £ on each £10,000 up to a maximum of £70,000. This is as far as Mr Zorn has carried his Tables. But it is evident that a fifth speed gear could be added for incomes exceeding £70,000, though in this highest reach some break must be put on the rate of progression so as to prevent the highest practicable limit of taxation being reached before the largest income is included. For as we approach the highest range of incomes with our taxing instrument we shall be confronted with the difficulty, betrayed in the case of the excess-profits tax, of the dissipation of potential income in expenses of management, bonuses to employees, and various other devices for evading high taxation. Moreover, in the highest incomes we are likely to encounter a cosmopolitan spirit on the part of their owners which may lead them to shift their domiciles and transfer their investments from one taxable area into another where a lower pressure of taxation is applied. Neither of these considerations precludes a high taxation on large incomes, but it places some restrictions upon the proportion of the 'surplus' which can be taken by the taxing authority for revenue. Since all these 'monstrous' incomes must in the nature of the case be derived from economic monopolies of a large and highly organized shape, it may well be the case that the State can attach their profits more successfully by nationalization than by taxation.

FIRST STAGE

		Tax in £.	Tax on respective £100.	Average Rate in £ of Tax over total Income.	Total Tax payable.	Percentage of Income payable.
1st	£100	/3	£1 5 0	/3	£1 5 0	1.25
2nd	100	/6	2 10 0	/4½	3 15 0	1.87
3rd	100	/9	3 15 0	/6	7 10 0	2.5
4th	100	1/–	5 0 0	/7½	12 10 0	3.12
5th	100	1/3	6 5 0	/9	18 15 0	3.75

EXAMPLE:—What is the tax on a taxable income of £365?

On	1st £100	.	.	.	.	.	£1 5 0
"	2nd 100	.	.	.	.	.	2 10 0
"	3rd 100	.	.	.	.	.	3 15 0
"	last 65	.	.	.	.	.	3 5 0

Total £10 15 0

An average of just over 7d. and 2.94 of the total income.

SECOND STAGE.—INCOMES of £600 to £1000.

The tax progresses successively by 6d. in the £1 on every additional £100 of Income.

	Tax in £.	Tax on respective £100.	Average rate in £ of Tax over total Income.	Total Tax payable.	Percentage of Income payable.
6th £100	1/9	£8 15 0	-/11	£27 10 0	4.58
7th 100	2/3	11 5 0	1/1	38 15 0	5.53
8th 100	2/9	13 15 0	1/3¾	52 10 0	6.56
9th 100	3/3	16 5 0	1/6	68 15 0	7.63
10th 100	3/9	18 15 0	1/9	87 10 0	8.75

EXAMPLE:—What is the tax on an income of £823?

On £800 . . . £52 10 0 An average of 1/3¾.
" £ 23 . . . 3 14 9 At 3/3 in £.

Total . . £56 4 9 An average of just over 1/4¼.

THIRD STAGE.—£1000 to £10,000.

	Tax in £.	Tax on respective £1000.	Average rate in £ of Tax over total Income.	Total Tax payable.	Percentage of Income payable.
1st £1000	1/9	£87 10 0	1/9	£87 10 0	8.75
2nd 1000	2/9	137 10 0	2/3	225 0 0	11.25
3rd 1000	3/9	187 10 0	2/9	412 10 0	13.75
4th 1000	4/9	237 10 0	3/3	650 0 0	16.25
5th 1000	5/9	287 10 0	3/9	937 10 0	18.75
6th 1000	6/9	337 10 0	4/3	1275 0 0	21.25
7th 1000	7/9	387 10 0	4/9	1662 10 0	23.75
8th 1000	8/9	437 10 0	5/3	2100 10 0	26.25
9th 1000	9/9	487 10 0	5/9	2587 10 0	28.75
10th 1000	10/9	537 10 0	6/3	3125 0 0	31.25

FOURTH STAGE.—£10,000 TO £70,000.

	Tax in £	Tax on respective £1000.	Average rate in £ of Tax over total Income.	Total Tax payable.	Percentage of Income payable.
1st £10,000	6/3	£3,125	6/3	£3,125	31.25
2nd 10,000	7/6	3,750	6/10½	6,875	34.37
3rd 10,000	8/9	4,375	7/6	11,250	37.5
4th 10,000	10/-	5,000	8/1½	16,250	40.62
5th 10,000	11/3	5,625	8/9	21,875	42.75
6th 10,000	12/6	6,250	9/4½	28,125	46.87
7th 10,000	13/9	6,875	10/-	35,000	50

CHAPTER V

REFORMS OF INCOME-TAX

§ 1. A proposal to cancel the discrimination in the taxation of earned and unearned incomes will doubtless arouse strong opposition. In order to justify it I must show that the ability to pay does not substantially differ in the two cases. But I would point out at the outset that the Income-Tax Commissioners, in distinguishing all interest as unearned, and as therefore possessing a higher ability to pay than the high income of a business man from profits, or of a professional man from fees, are resting upon two quite erroneous suppositions. The first is contained in the curious adoption of the Socialist view of all interest as 'unearned,' in the sense that its production involves no personal effort or sacrifice on the recipient. Now, under an economic system, when saving has to be effected by inducing individuals to forgo certain amounts of present enjoyment which their incomes would enable them to procure, in order to bring into existence and maintain in productive use the means and instruments of future production, a good deal of the saving and the maintenance of capital does involve a postponement of present enjoyment and an effort of will on the part of certain classes of investors which, as we have seen, requires a minimum rate of interest to be regarded as a 'cost of production.' Though the effect of this abstinence may be negligible in the case of the rich, while the rate of interest actually obtained may often be larger than is required to evoke what effort is involved in saving, it is distinctly untrue that all interest is 'unearned' within any meaning reasonably attributable to that term. On the other hand, as we have seen, a great deal of other income which comes to the well-to-do classes, as profits, wages of management, salaries and fees, is 'unearned,' in the sense that it consists of excessive payments for goods or services, obtained by the restraint of free effective competition, and unnecessary to evoke the use of the personal productive services which are supposed to have earned it. It is, in effect, the rent of inequality of opportunity just as much as is the differential rent of land, and has no more title to be regarded as earned. The fact that it is associated with some voluntary productive activity on the part of a business or professional man does not affect this judgment. A very large proportion of the upper strata of these incomes can be taken in income-tax without causing any withdrawal or reduced efficiency of the productive services rendered by the recipients. Because a big business profiteer is able to 'earn' £50,000 a year by applying his brains and knowledge to his opportunities, it does not follow that the removal of half of it, or more, by income taxation would induce him to work less efficiently, or to go earlier out of business. He takes all he can, but there is no warrant for supposing that all he gets is needed to evoke his business efforts. So, too, with the high-salaried manager or the successful professional man who earns his £20,000 a year. He sells his skill and ability at the highest price he can get in a market where he enjoys a scarcity-position by means of his personal reputation or the special opportunities he has enjoyed. The notion that, because he can command this salary or these fees, he can and will resist taxation by refusing to do his work, is baseless. It rests on an utterly false estimate of his position and psychology. If we were to put high taxation on large legal incomes and not upon large incomes in medicine or engineering, it is evident that fewer able and enterprising men would enter the former profession, and the growing scarcity of this ability would raise legal fees, so throwing off on to other people the discriminative taxation. And so it would be with all similar discrimination. But if all high 'earned' incomes, irrespective of the particular business or profession, were equally subjected to high taxation, no such scarcity of competing ability would be produced and no consequent escape from the taxation. There is no inherent virtue or power in a particular sort of capacity or skill to compel the public to pay an exceedingly high price for it, and to enable the recipient to resist all attempts to diminish it by taxation. A great lawyer may make £20,000 a year in England, whereas an equally great lawyer might make only £5000 in Switzerland, Sweden, or even France. Why? For two contributory causes, first, because wider access to education and the professions in the latter countries implies a larger supply of high-grade legal ability; secondly, because the general distribution of wealth is more equal in these countries so that there are fewer persons able to pay the higher fees that prevail here. Perhaps a third consideration may be added, the higher general level of intelligence and knowledge in such countries as Switzerland, Holland or France, operating to reduce the purely superstitious part of a professional reputation. At any rate, the fact is certain that equally good professional and business capacity can be obtained in different countries at widely different levels of remuneration. This means that large professional and business incomes often enjoy a proportionately large rent of ability which is a true economic rent in its inability to resist taxation by a curtailment of supply. The fact that some personal productive effort is put forth in earning this must not be allowed to blind us to the recognition that the excessive portion of the payment for it is as much unearned as the ground rent of a landowner or the monopoly interest of a trust-magnate.

When, therefore, proper provisions have been made for exempting all low incomes from taxation and for splitting small or moderate family incomes into individual incomes for purposes of exemption or taxation, there remains no just reason for

maintaining a distinction between earned and unearned incomes, which complicates the theory and
application of a really scientific income-tax. Indeed, the abandonment of the differentiation by
our Income-Tax Law in the higher levels of income (for the lower rate for earned income only
extends to the £2500 level) may be taken as an
admission of the substance of our case.

§ 2. Equally indefensible is the exemption from
income-tax of investments which rank under the
head of Life Insurance policies. There is no just
presumption that A, by paying annual premiums
to an Insurance Company, in order to provide for
his family in case of his demise, is making a better
use of his income than B, who invests his money
for the same purpose in Consols or other gilt-
edged securities, or than C, who spends the money
upon a good education for his children or in estab-
lishing them on a good professional or business
footing. The preference is based upon a narrow
and short-sighted notion of economy. There is
no ground for applying a special incentive to induce persons to save rather than to spend, irrespective of the nature of the spending and of the
investment of the savings. Still less is it desirable to stimulate by a special bonus the saving
of the poorer classes, whose income does not usu-

ally suffice for a current expenditure sufficient to bring up a family in full human efficiency. National Economy demands that the maximum amount of saving should be done by the well-to-do whose saving involves no trenching upon serviceable expenditure, the minimum by the classes who have to 'pinch' in order to save. Still less defensible is the preference given to Life Insurance Companies over other investment companies in respect of the portions of premiums which support what are termed Endowment Policies, or earn bonuses or other pecuniary gains which can be taken by the subscriber during his lifetime.

§ 3. If the income-tax is to be made a completely effective instrument of public revenue, everything that rightly ranks as income must come within its operation. Two large forms of income escape proper assessment under the existing operation of the tax. No attempt has hitherto been made at direct assessment of farmers' profits under Schedule B. Assessed at one-third of the annual value before the war, the great majority were virtually exempt from all payment, their so-called profits, measured by this deceptive standard, falling below the exemption limit or contributing a negligible sum. In the first decade of this century the total 'profit from the occupation of land' never reached five million pounds, and the actual contribution of this class of income to the revenue seldom exceeded a quarter of a million pounds. During the war the basis of assessment for farmers' profits was raised to the full annual value. But even this advance is a ridiculously inadequate measure of the true level of profits. In 1816-17 the total income taxed upon this basis amounted to £16,389,972, while the net yield of the tax was £2,850,121. It must also be borne in mind that the excess-profits tax was not made applicable to profits of agriculture, though the enormous rise of food prices, guaranteed for years to come by the Corn Production Act, raised agriculture to a condition of unprecedented prosperity. Special difficulties beset the process of assessment in this class of income. The farmer and his dependents are in large measure maintained directly from the proceeds of the farm, and this 'real' income is difficult to ascertain and value. Sound book-keeping is hard for farmers, and is seldom attempted. But these difficulties are not insuperable. Skilled accountancy is essential to successful modern farming, and farmers should be required to conform to the rules of book-keeping necessary to disclose their real income, employing competent outside assistance if they are not equal to the task themselves. For a long time to come agricultural prices and profits will be very high, and it is intolerable that 'the agricultural interests' should be permitted to make money out of food shortage while escaping their proper contribution to the revenue.

§ 4. It is likely that in the skilled and in some of the more strenuous of the unskilled trades there are many families whose annual incomes possess a taxable capacity. The labour shortage in the war, co-operating with other pressures, brought a rise both of money and of real income to some grades of workers which in many instances may be permanent. Many wage-earning families should figure in the lower levels of the income-tax payers, and adequate measures should be taken to secure their contribution. It should, however, be kept clearly in mind that in their case, as in others, the contribution is based upon, and measured by, ability to pay, i.e. the possession of some surplus-income beyond the needs of family efficiency. The belief that great numbers of working-class incomes in ordinary times escape the income-tax they ought to pay has no foundation in fact. Dr J. S. Stamp, in his authoritative work on "British Incomes and Property," speaks of "the popular notion that many little workers on weekly wages escape,'' and makes the following comment: ''In the first place, the number who *sustain* an average of over £3 per week continuously over three years, without a break, is not large. At any given time there may be a considerable number above the margin, but they are not the same cases continuously. Secondly, machinery was provided in 1907 as adequate to secure the greater part of the real liability. Thirdly, with the children's allowances, abatements, etc., the loss in *duty* is very small.'' The argument, so constantly urged, that the workers ought to pay direct taxes, however small, in order that they may realize the responsibilities of citizenship, rests on a wholly erroneous conception of the relation of citizens towards the State and of the nature of State revenue. For when once it is realized that those surplus-elements of income which taxation collects are really social earnings, the product of social activities and needs, and not 'sacrifices' imposed upon citizens whose 'property' is confiscated for public ends, it will be seen to be unjust and foolish to attempt any encroachment upon the earnings of any family that are required to maintain the full efficiency of its members. If, as is likely, in the future large numbers of manual workers earn incomes as large as the lower grades of professional and official workers, a considerable amount of revenue may legitimately be drawn from their 'surplus.' This consideration, however, should give urgency to a reform in the regulation of the exemption level. Considering that the distinction between taxable and untaxable incomes ultimately rests upon real and not money income, provisions should be made for an automatic adjustment of the exemption level to the fluctuations of price level.

§5. The adoption of the taxable capacity of the family income as the true basis for a scientific income-tax demands a reconsideration of the strongly established usage of 'collection at the source.' More than three-quarters of tax, it is estimated, is thus intercepted in the way of deductions from the interest, rents, profits and salaries, from public funds and offices, joint-stock companies and other 'public' bodies. Official opinion has hitherto been persistent in its assertion of the importance of maintaining this method of assessment and collection. It would, no doubt, be possible to retain this method under a reformed tax, in which every income paid a different amount and in which account was taken of the number of dependents on an income. But the balance would seem to turn heavily against such retention. For,

whereas at present the 6s. tax deducted at source
on unearned income has only to be adjusted by
way of abatements or exemptions to meet the case
of small or moderate incomes, under a scientific
graduation there could be no tax fixed at 6s. or
at any other rate, but a tax-curve calculated so
as to yield an average of, say, 6s., though that
precise amount was paid by a negligible number
of incomes.   To fix upon an arbitrary or an average sum, such as 6s., to deduct it from the source,
and then to make an infinite number of separate
additions and deductions to meet the case of all
the actual incomes, would prove an intolerable
task.   Moreover, with the necessity of reckoning
the tax rate for each separate large personal income would disappear the security for the full
payment of the tax in the case of large incomes
that is afforded by the present method.   It should
be kept in mind that the official convenience of collection at the source is the chief reason why the
process of progressive graduation has hitherto
been stopped at a level which has protected the
richest men from the higher taxation which they
possess ability to bear.   So long as taxation at
the source is adhered to, this injurious wastage
must continue, for it is not feasible to fix the tax
rate to accord with the highest incomes, and the

separate super-tax imposed is at best a clumsy remedy.

Since true ability to pay can only be measured by the separate individual income, no good purpose can be serve by taking what is *ex hypothesi* a false basis for assessment and collection. Now that the State needs the maximum revenue obtainable, it must set itself to the measurement and checking of the separate personal incomes which contain the taxable *corpus*. So long as a very large proportion of taxpayers were under no obligation or inducement to make a complete return of income from all sources, the case for taxation at the source was a strong one. But it has already been much weakened by the extension of abatements, differentiations, allowances and exemptions, and by the provisions for the super-tax. It is now estimated that something like 99 per cent. of all the incomes come under individual survey, involving a separate assessment in each case. It is quite evidently the duty of the Government to require every person with a taxable income to present the State with a complete annual account of his income.

§ 6. It will doubtless be contended that, if one graduated tax be substituted for the existing system with its numerous deductions and abatements, the motives, operative at present to evoke a full return from persons claiming their allowances, will cease to operate, and it will be difficult to prevent under-statements and evasions of the tax. The idea of a total abandonment of collection at the source need not, however, cause any great alarm, provided that the official information available by access to governmental and company accounts is utilized to check the individual returns upon which assessment is made. What is needed is a simplified and standardized form of account to be kept by the taxpayer in his annual dealing with the State, so as to enable the latter to ascertain the net annual income of the tax-payer. With the abolition of the needlessly complicated Schedules of the present tax and its differentiations, allowances, etc., the task of the taxpayer would be greatly reduced. Careful instructions should be given upon the distributions between gross and net income, and free official assistance should be available for those who seek it in making out and presenting their account. Moreover, the growing volume of information relating to individual incomes derivable from the returns of companies and private business firms should be utilized in order to check the individual returns of income.

The Inland Revenue has, I understand, already given up taxation at the source for almost all dividends payable at the Bank of England. By requiring complete detailed returns from the paying companies, they could follow the same course in the case of other dividends. The information thus supplied could be used to check failures of individual returns. Each year a mixed assortment of Company returns could be made the basis of a close scrutiny into the returns made by the recipients of interest, profits and other payments, and sharp penalties applied to all cases of defalcation or gross negligence. I would urge that the sham-sanctity of bank accounts should be abolished,[1] and that the pass-book should become an ordinary recognized source of official information upon incomes. A careful application of these checks would enable the Income-Tax Commissioners to dispense with collection at the source and to place the tax upon its proper individual footing. The stiff official bluff which will be put up on behalf of the present method by the Treasury, supported by the *ipse dixit* of certain expert authorities, must not be permitted to block the way to

---

[1] The Government has not scrupled during the last few years to force upon Banks, under the Defence of the Realm Act, an exposure of many private accounts.

the adoption of the only scientific working of an income-tax.

CHAPTER VI

DEATH DUTIES

§ 1. The relation between the Income-Tax and the group of taxes upon Estates, Probate, Legacies and Succession, commonly designated Death Duties, is one of intimacy and importance. For the two forms of taxation are both complementary and substitutional. The capital wealth that passes at death may be regarded as the accumulation of wealth which has figured in the income of the deceased or some predecessor, and has not been spent or taken in taxation. Though certain special instances of increment of capital value, viz., profits on the sale of ships and on the sale of controlled establishments have recently been brought within the income-tax, a great deal of these gains will have escaped entirely the incidence of taxation when they came into existence. For there are various additions to the wealth which a man may obtain within a given year that lie outside the purview of the Inland Revenue Authorities. A landowner may find the value of his land growing every year, but that growth escapes taxation, though it is an enlargement of his income for all effective purposes. No attempt at all is made to levy taxation upon certain other increments of capital value, such as rises in the market value of securities, or profit from their sale, or from deductions from gross business earnings which under the head of renewals, reserves, etc., enhance the capital value of a business, or from various windfalls that lie outside the routine operations of the business. Various forms of what is termed 'cutting the melon,' *i.e.* distribution of gains outside the ordinary declaration of dividends, are devised for the purpose of escaping publicity and income-tax. Sometimes this takes shape in 'bonuses,' sometimes in duplication of shares, sometimes in preferential terms for the taking up of new share capital. In periods of rapid industrial and commercial growth and in periods of turmoil, when speculative enterprise and rapid strategic finance find favourable scope, an immense quantity of fresh values escape from ever figuring as taxable income. It is, of course, true that the annual interest, rent or profit, which this enhanced wealth procures for its owner may pay income-tax. But the *corpus* itself, though at some time or another it came as an addition to the year's gain of the owner, was not taxed as income in that or any other year.

§ 2. Here, then, is a large body of wealth, composed almost entirely of accidental monopoly or preferential gains, that forms a surplus peculiarly fitted for taxation. Some of it ought without doubt to be brought under the operation of the income-tax. An annual tax upon capital, and a periodical levy upon capital increment, are proposals that have some support from experiments in other countries. But a strong case can be made out for retaining the Death Duties as the chief supplement to a scientific Income-Tax, and for enlarging them so as to claim for the public revenue a very large share of the wealth passing at the demise of its owner.

For our analysis of income, with its distinction between 'costs' and 'surplus,' was based upon a progressive and not a statical conception of the industrial system. It, therefore, contemplated the necessity, under private business enterprise, of large additions to the capital structure made out of the savings from individual incomes. Now this 'voluntary' saving from ordinary income, though largely consisting of the 'automatic' accumulation of large unspent elements of income, probably requires to be supplemented by a good deal of saving which is not automatic, but calculated and inspired by the desire for interest or profit. This consideration imposes some limit upon the height of an income-tax which shall include as taxable income the whole of 'saved' as well as 'spent' income. Now there are grounds for holding that the 'savings' on an income will be more sensitive to taxation than the spendings, in the sense that a very high tax would cause in them a far larger shrinkage. Believing, as I do, that at the present economic juncture it will be necessary to take what measures are necessary to evoke a higher proportion of saving to spending than prevailed before the war, and that some considerable part of this saving must be done by persons of moderate income, I think that if our single graduation income-tax is to be the chief financial instrument it must not press unduly upon the savings of these classes. If it could be done without excessive sacrifice of current revenue and with adequate safeguards against abuse, I should be disposed to give favourable consideration to a proposal for exempting from assessment a certain percentage of all incomes, above the true family subsistence level, and below the present super-tax level, on condition of its investment in Government or other securities, public or private, authorized by Commissioners who were guided by a large public policy in the direction of the flow of capital.

If this proposition seems to some an unwarranted concession to capitalism, I would remind such critics that this suggested remission does not involve a corresponding loss to the public revenue, but chiefly a postponement. It is based upon the conviction that for the furtherance of national productivity, a certain stimulus of private gain is needed to evoke the necessary amount of saving from individual owners of income. This necessary saving can be evoked either by a high rate of interest or by a remission of taxation, or by a blend of the two. The proposal, however, is not an indiscriminate remission which would subsidize all capitalists by enabling them to get the use of capital cheapened by what amounted to a public subsidy. It involves a public direction and preferential treatment of savings applied to useful public purposes, *e.g.* housing, electric extension, etc., or to the urgent increase of productive plant in essential industries.

Such an exemption, were it adopted, would, I repeat, not involve much loss of revenue. In fact, if it were the best mode of evoking a more adequate flow of new savings, there would be no ultimate loss, but probably a gain. For though the saved income would not be taxed at the time of saving, the interest it earned as capital would be brought under the ordinary income-tax, while the capital itself would be taxed on the death of the owner. If the policy, in other words, were economically productive, the State would partake of the productivity.

§ 3. But whether this proposal for remission of taxation on authorized new saving be acceptable or not, it is certainly expedient to secure that the income-tax shall not be so heavy as unduly to interfere with the saving of the classes who can afford to save. Now the excessively heavy income-tax might do this in one of two ways, or in both. It might cause that part of the income which otherwise would have been saved to be expended in maintaining the established standard of comfort. Or it might even deter a person from earning the highest income he is capable of earning, causing him to withdraw the productive effort involved in earning that part of his income which was unnecessary to maintain his normal expenditure. There are no doubt compensating forces to be taken into account. There is a case for high taxation as a stimulus to industry. Some men will be so bent upon preserving their usual standard both of expenditure and saving against the encroachments of the tax-gatherer that they will work harder or better in order to obtain the same net income after payment of the higher tax. But there will be a physical and moral limit to this stimulus. A small or moderate encroachment by the State upon their former income may be met by an increased output of productive energy, but each new increment of this energy will be attended by a higher personal cost, and a large encroachment could only be met, if at all, by an injurious and ultimately an uneconomical strain. Even where no great personal effort is involved in earning, the experience of this war, especially in regard to the war-profits tax, affords abundant evidence that very high taxation checks, not stimulates, very high production.

§ 4. Summing up the argument, I hold it established that a sound taxing-system will treat an income-tax and death duties as complementary methods of securing for the State the maximum revenue from surplus wealth. Death duties are serviceable not merely as a net for catching those parts of unearned or surplus wealth which have escaped the income-tax. Their chief service is that they enable the income-tax to be kept normally within such reasonable limits as not to check

the immediate earning energy, or the saving, of
any class of the community. This is, of course,
attributable partly to the fact that a man is ordinarily less concerned about what will happen to
his property after he is dead than about what
will happen during his lifetime. But a good deal
is also attributable to the curious illusion which
leads so many men to think, feel and act as if they
were going to live for ever. They simply refuse
to 'realize' their death or to take account of it in
the play of economic motives that affect their
earning and saving. Putting the matter con-
cretely, I do not believe that well-to-do people
would accumulate and leave behind them less than
they do now, if the State were to take one-half
or more of their estates instead of the tenth which
it now takes on an average.

Nor is it merely the case that the persons who
leave the property are not greatly affected in their
motives by a high death duty. The recipients of
the residue, receiving it as a sudden or fortuitous
addition to their own resources, easily acquiesce
in large deductions from the windfall. Apart
from this, the general attitude of the public, especially in America and Britain, has become certainly more favourable to this method of raising
revenue. Even the well-to-do are less concerned

than formerly to make large provisions for heirs and dependents, and the general atmosphere of the modern world is unfavourable to the idea of great estates or businesses as heirlooms. Viewed from the social-economic standpoint, the heavy taxation of hereditary fortunes which enable and encourage their recipients to live in idleness, and by their expenditure to draw large numbers of workers into luxury trades and services, is a double gain.

From these considerations it follows that every enlargement of the income-tax should be accompanied by a corresponding enlargement of death duties, partly, as an alternative, curtailing the excess of the former, partly as a supplement tapping the same wealth more conveniently later on.

CHAPTER VII

SUPPLEMENTARY TAXES

§ 1. Taking 'ability to pay' as our criterion, we have so far confined our consideration to the general forms of taxation based upon the presumption that 'ability to pay' varies directly with the amount of income or of wealth. But incorporated in our existing revenue system are other imposts, resting partly upon other special tests of 'ability,' partly upon considerations of public welfare other than the purely fiscal.

First, we may take the case of taxes upon superfluities or luxuries. Under this head I should place the Inhabited House Duty, which is still curiously attached to our Income-Tax, figuring as a second informal income-tax based upon a supposition that 'ability to pay' can be measured by gross or net rental of houses. Regarded as a secondary income-tax, it is utterly indefensible. The relation between taxable income and rental of a dwelling-house is too loose to be of any value for national taxation. The tax penalizes town dwellers for the benefit of country dwellers, ignores the fundamental consideration of the number of dependents on an income requiring house-room, stops its graduations at £60 a year, thus leaving the ordinary middle-class family to pay as high a proportion as the solitary dweller in a palace, and ignores the best test of superfluous housing, viz., the occupation of a second or third house by the rich.

Now having regard to the fact that the income-tax is admittedly an incomplete instrument, based on a presumption and not a direct measure of ability to pay, I find a strong case for reinforcing it by a few taxes upon luxuries. Foremost among these I would place an Inhabited House Tax, reconstructed for the purpose. The first and most obvious reform would be the restriction of the tax to dwellings where the accommodation in space and number of rooms was more than adequate to the hygienic and other reasonable needs of the family in occupation. This would in many cases, perhaps in most, imply a raising of the exemption limit in towns to considerably above £20, the present limit, thus offering a proportionate encouragement to the building and renting of decent houses for the working and lower middle-class families. The other reforms of this tax would accord with the general revision of the income-tax. The abrupt increase of tax-rate at £40 and £60 would be replaced by a smooth graduation which would continue until the highest rental was reached. Occupiers of more than one house would be taxed not upon the lower level of each separate rental, but upon the basis of the aggregate rental of all the premises they held for occupation.

§ 2. How far other specific luxury taxes should be retained or imposed depends upon a variety of considerations, not entirely fiscal. In fact, the purely fiscal will in most cases be a minor factor.

For the net yield of most luxury taxes cannot be very great when the cost and trouble of assessment and collection are taken into account. There will always remain a just presumption against interfering with the liberty of persons in the expenditure of their income. Only a few instances may this presumption be outweighed by net considerations of public utility. One of these considerations is the fact that such a tax is already in operation and the instruments of its collection already exist. For this reason, among others, it may be worth while to retain the existing licence duties upon motor-cars and carriages, men-servants, game licences, and such minor luxuries as armorial bearings, though the aggregate yield of such taxation is small. A few of the minor long-established licence duties of wider incidence, such as those on guns and dogs, may be retained, not for purposes of revenue, but as checks upon luxurious consumption and on grounds of public order. But new and vexatious taxes, such as the public performance duty, and some older stamp duties, like that on playing cards, should disappear.

The only important indirect taxes which an intelligent State would retain are those directed to the control and restraint of a few important

articles of popular luxury, the large consumption
of which is not merely a presumption of the possession of superfluous income, but is definitely
detrimental to personal health, morals or public
order. Of this character are alcoholic drinks and
tobacco, in the dimensions of their present use.
Though the taxes and licences applied to their
case are often unfair and unreasonable in their
proportions, incidence and methods of collection,
a substantial body of taxation may rightly be imposed upon them, directed so as to repress or even
extinguish the more detrimental forms of drink-
ing. All the other indirect taxes, under the heads
of Customs or Excise, Licence or Stamp duties,
should be removed, except so far as they consist
of registration fees carrying some advantage of
security or preference to the payee. The so-called
Breakfast duties, taxes upon tea, coffee, cocoa,
sugar, are an indefensible secret assault upon the
meagre incomes of the poor, upon which they
impose a far heavier proportionate burden than
upon the rich. The disproportionate burden on
the poor from the Breakfast table and other indirect taxation is so heavy as to outweigh the exemption of such incomes from direct taxation.
This is clearly shown in the valuable analysis presented by Mr Herbert Scammel in his recent

Presidential Address to the Royal Statistical Society on "The Taxation of Various Classes of the People." His conclusion from the figures he cites is as follows:—

"The columns of percentages in the tables show that the British system of taxation is regressive in the lower stages; the classes with the smallest incomes pay a larger proportion of them in contributions to the revenue than the classes immediately above them. This inequality was very marked in the first period we have had under consideration (i.e. 1903-4). It had been redressed a little, but only a little, during the decade before the war. It still persists, though the disappearance of any considerable class in the community, with family incomes of only £1 a week, has gone far to lessen the disparity. Such regression is the consequence of relying for revenue upon the taxation of alcohol, tobacco, tea and sugar, and of the fact that the consumption of these articles is larger in proportion to income among the poorer classes" (p. 38).

In pre-war times Chancellors boggled about this urgently pressed reform on grounds of national economy, grudging the few millions loss of revenue which their removal would entail. But in any such reconstruction of national finance as we here contemplate, and having regard to the magnitude of the new demands, such short-sighted niggling economy can hardly be defended. But in itself, such secret taxation is doubly injurious when it deprives the poorer families of a sufficient consumption of articles of prime utility.

§ 3. From what we have said, it follows that any general luxury tax, such as that contemplated and prepared by our Government in 1918, is to be condemned. A sound fiscal system will strike at luxurious expenditure, primarily by taking, through income-tax and death duties, the superfluous income available for expenditure on luxuries, supporting this attack by a few specific taxes upon large forms of class or popular luxuries, selected either for their representative character and large yield, as in the case of inhabited house duty and motor-cars, or for reasons related to the wasteful or detrimental nature of high consumption, as in the case of alcohol. To any such general luxury tax, as was proposed, every fault adheres. It is a vexatious interference with liberty of individual taste, involves infinite trouble to the seller and the buyer, is incalculable in its real incidence and repercussions, is highly susceptible of evasion, and is very difficult of definition. It may be taken as the *reductio ad absurdum* of indirect taxation.

§ 4. A more important issue is raised by the existence of a large number of Stamp duties, some of which have been created or increased during the period of the war. These duties can mostly be classed for convenience under four heads:[1]

I. Taxes on bills of exchange and promissory notes.

II. A penny (or two-penny) tax on receipts, cheques, drafts, etc.

III. Taxes on transactions relating to property such as sales, settlements of money leases and securities for money.

IV. Taxes on deeds and other instruments.

A fifth class may be added consisting of fees for admission to branches of the legal profession and to various other offices or for acts of a quasi-official character. The great majority of these duties consist of taxes upon transfer of money or other property incidental to the conduct of ordinary 'business' operations. An analysis of the yield of such taxation in a normal year shows that these deeds of disposal or transfer of property, including forms of conveyance, receipts, drafts,

[1] See "The King's Revenue," by W. M. J. Williams, p. 101.

cheques, bills of exchange, insurance policies, share certificates, contract notes, marketable securities, bankers' bills and notes, share warrants, etc., cover nine-tenths of the total amount raised from stamps. Now the whole of this, with the exception of the small fees required to cover the cost of official registration, is levied in restraint of trade or of other forms of presumable personal and social utility. In some instances the operation of these duties upon transfer of property is such as to inflict grave injustice. This is the case when a property is bought with borrowed money, or is paid for by instalments. When a man buys a house worth £500 with £50 only of his own money, borrowing the rest, it is exceedingly hard that he should be called upon to pay a £10 tax, the same amount he would have paid if the whole purchase money were his own.

The only excuse for levying such taxes has been that they form, as a rule, a very small proportion of the total value exchanging hands. Where, however, the values transferred are themselves small, they not infrequently constitute an enormous burden upon the payee, and a real interference with freedom of purchase or other business arrangement. It is clearly to the public interest that all such fees should be kept at a cost of registration level, and that the State should not set itself to extort any income from such sources. The few millions (less than eight in the year 1908) derived from these stamps are, in their final incidence, at the best nothing but an expensive way of tapping certain bits of income, which, left untapped, would yield their quota to ordinary direct taxation, while at their worst they are extortions from persons who possess no real ability to pay. For the most part they are the cumbersome relics of a past haphazard method of catchpenny improvisation which has no place in any scientific system of finance.

CHAPTER VIII

TARIFFS FOR REVENUE

§ 1. The acceptance of our principle that surplus-income is the only fund containing ability to bear taxation relieves us of the necessity of entering into the lengthy and various controversy recently revived in this country about the financial and economic effects of protective and preferential tariffs upon imports. For the supporters of a tariff on imports base their case on the assumption or assertion that the foreigner can be made to pay. If, and so far as he can be made to pay, there is a strong *prima facie* case for such a tariff as will make him pay as much as possible. But whether and how much can be got out of him depends, according to our accepted principle, upon whether he has some surplus income on which we can levy our import duty.

Now just as we have found in our own industries many processes of production or distribution in which some monopolist or combination has a 'pull' that enables him to get a price for his goods or services containing 'surplus,' we may rightly assume, and experience confirms the assumption, that the foreign industries making some of the sorts of goods which we import will be subject at some stage of production or transport or marketing to similar pulls which earn surplus income for the business firms that exercise them. There have been cartels and trusts in Germany and the United States exporting to this country portions of their output at cheaper prices than they get at home for the goods they market there, and earning from the aggregate of their receipts an income containing considerable surplus. Can we get at this by putting an import tariff on their goods entering our ports? It is not obvious that we can. For the goods 'dumped' on us are as-

sumed, often rightly, to be sold at below what
would be their cost price if a separate cost could
be assigned to their production. The profitable
part of the output which yields the surplus is that
part sold in the home market of the exporting
cartel or firm. Are we able by putting a tax on
the 'dumped' goods to get it out of the surplus
profits made from the sale of the undumped
goods? No simple general answer can be given.
It will not do to say that any tax so imposed must
cause a stoppage of the dumping. Such dumping
belongs to the economy of large production. A
strong trust, combine or cartel, controlling its
home market (sometimes by a tariff wall, sometimes not) finds that it can produce at a lower
cost per unit of the output by producing at a faster
rate than the home market will take without a
large lowering of price. It finds it more profitable
upon the whole to restrict its sales and maintain
high prices, with a wide margin of profit in the
market over which it has direct control, 'dumping'
the residue on outside markets. For any price it
can get? Not so. A little reflection makes it
evident that the price for the dumped stock is
an important factor in the total economy of the
procedure. It would not pay them to 'give away'
their surplus stock in order to maintain the output

which can be produced at the lowest cost per unit. An article sold in America at $1 might be 'dumped' in this country at 75 cents. But it by no means follows that if we put on a 25 cent duty it would be shifted on to them.

The British importer, as usual, would be called upon to pay the duty on receipt of the goods in our ports. Since he presumably could not bear the tax, he would doubtless try to shift it on to the foreign exporter or manufacturer by stopping further orders, except at a price reduced by the 25 cents. Would he get this reduction, the goods entering as before and paying the import duty from foreign surplus? Only upon two assumptions. The first is that there was no other country to which the dumping could be transferred, at some sacrifice of price less than 25 per cent. The probability is that the dumper would find some such other dumping ground for his surplus stock. In that event the tariff brings no money to our revenue, while it enables our own producers of these goods to raise the price to our consumers up to a limit of 25 per cent. The other assumption is that the policy of the American combine or the German cartel remains unaffected, so far as the economy of large output goes, by our new tariff, *i.e.* that it will still pay them to sell the same quantity of goods at a higher price in their own market, and dump the same surplus upon us. But this will hardly ever be the case. The normal result of the reduced sum obtainable from their dumping would be, either to cause them to enlarge their home market by lowering their prices, or to reduce their total output by shutting down their least effective plant and labour.

§ 2. There will be rare instances in which it might still pay the foreigner to continue dumping, and to bear out of his aggregate surplus profits at least a portion of the import duty. Where the dumper had a virtual monopoly of some product for which he could find no other dumping ground, and which he could not unload at home without a great reduction of price, while any reduction of output would be accompanied by no reduction of overhead costs, the dumper might bear some or even all the tax, subsidizing his dumped goods out of the high profits of his home market. There may be cases, if our Government could know enough about the trade in question to calculate their deli-cate chances, where a tariff might 'make the foreigner pay.' These cases would all hinge upon two conditions. One is that the economy of costs of production forces the foreign producers to an output considerably larger than he can profitably market in his own country, so that a foreign dumping ground is necessary to enable him to earn his highest aggregate profit. The other condition is that the taxing-system in the foreign country is so lax as to allow a foreign Treasury to take by taxation a surplus which it could itself secure for the upkeep of the State of which the producers were citizens. If the Government of a country in which a monopoly operates gainfully refrains from taking its share of the gains got from overcharging its consumers, it is economically feasible for the Government of another country which receives these monopoly-goods to take by means of import duties some portion of the monopoly-gain. It is possible that some part of a tax put upon American oil entering this country would be borne by the Standard Oil Trust. It is conceivable that a tax upon American meat might in some part fall upon the Big Five, and that the so-called Imperial Tobacco Trust might bear part of any special duty placed upon its American tobaccos. In these cases, however, there are still stricter limits upon the feasibility of making the foreigner pay than in the case of ordinary factory goods. For where raw materials form a large element in the costs of production, the law of differential rent is apt to interfere in the taxing process, by causing a withdrawal of the production of the materials, whether meat, tobacco or what not, grown on marginal land, *i.e.* land where it only just pays to grow them. Therefore it would be impossible for a foreign Government to get much out of any trust a tax upon the products of which would cause an automatic shrinkage of production, some land either being thrown out of cultivation or diverted to some other productive use.

This distinction between the taxibility of industries conforming respectively to the so-called laws of increasing and diminishing returns is well recognized by economists as limiting the power to apply a tariff so as to make the foreigner pay. Though differential rents of land have complete ability to bear taxation directly imposed upon them, and cannot shift such taxation, they cannot be reached by a tax imposed upon their produce. For, since some of this produce is raised on land yielding no such differential rent, a tax on the produce must drive such land out of use, reduce the supply of such produce, raise its price, and so transfer the tax to the consumer. Only in cases where there was such scarcity of land that the worst land contributing to the produce yielded a positive rent could any part of a tariff on this import fall upon the foreign landowner, and then only if a proportionate duty were put upon any other produce which this land could be made to yield.

If the entire overseas supply of any article entering this country were carried by some shipping combine which charged excessive freight rates, it might be possible to levy import duties which would fall upon this 'surplus,' but again subject to the two provisos: first, that there was no other country to which the goods could be conveyed and would fetch nearly as good a price; and secondly, that there was no other untaxed merchandise which could be substituted as a cargo.

These arguments will suffice to show that the ordinary notion that 'the foreigner will pay' the import duty is void of substance. The circumstances under which he would bear some portion of the duty are so rare and so incalculable that no Government officials could be safely entrusted with the adjustment of such a tariff. For if it is no easy task to arrange internal taxation so as to tap business surpluses made in this country under conditions fairly ascertainable, how much more difficult must it be to attempt to tap foreign surpluses made under conditions difficult to ascertain, and by the single indirect and usually futile method of a tax upon commodities?

Moreover, the attempt by means of import duties to poach upon the taxable funds of a foreign country is likely to be even less effective in the future than in the past. For the great foreign exporters of the manufactured goods which we import are nearly all members of countries pledged by the same exigencies of post-war finance as are operative here to a high and searching taxation of their own surplus incomes for their national revenue. It will be exceedingly unlikely that the United States or Germany, which possess powers to levy direct taxes upon the surplus profits of their monopolies and combinations, will leave much opportunity to us to reach these financial resources by the indirect method of import duties.

§ 3. It is pretty evident that import duties as a method of making 'the foreigner' contribute to our revenue are almost negligible. The well-known and general effect of such taxation is to throw the burden upon the consumer in enhanced prices of the goods he buys. Where the imports are raw materials, machinery or other costs of production in some British industry, organized so strongly as a trust or combine as to be able to earn surplus profits; the heightened price of such imports may of course be defrayed either wholly or in part from this surplus-income, and the ultimate consumer may not pay. For though the British trust or combine might be able to raise its selling prices and so transfer the burden to the ultimate consumer, it might not pay to do so, if the elasticity of the public demand were such that any further rise of prices would cause too great a shrinkage in demand. It is not likely, in any case, that any considerable amount of money could be thus collected by such indirect taxation upon surplus-incomes in this country which could not be reached better by direct taxation of income.

We must, therefore, come to the conclusion that import duties, whatever the orders of goods upon which they are placed, will ordinarily be paid by the ultimate consumer. This statement, of course, requires the qualification "if he has an income with some ability to bear the tax." For it still stands as the central truth in taxing theory that all taxes fall in the last resort on surplus-income. Therefore, if any class of consumer has no surplus-income capable of paying the higher prices caused by the import duty, the shifting process will begin, which we examined when we dealt with taxes on commodities as a method of internal finance. Indeed, the disturbance caused to industrial and social order by the efforts of consumers to shift high prices due to tariffs is one of the most serious damages of this bad system of finance. Of all forms of taxation tariff duties are the most injurious in their numerous, widespread and incalculable shiftings, in the delays and incidental injustice of their incidence, in the uncertainty of their yield, the costliness of their collection, and the business and political corruptions which they breed.

§ 4. Regarded as a supplementary method of gathering into the revenue such portions of surplus-income as have escaped direct taxation, a tariff is notoriously a clumsy instrument. The interest of all classes of business men is engaged in advance in evading it when it turns against them, and of exploiting it for their private gain when it can be turned against any other business interest or, in particular, the consumer. When it falls on the consumer, as is normally the case, it imposes on him a tax far exceeding the revenue passing to the exchequer. For, by enabling the protected trades in this country to raise their prices nearly to the amount of the import duty, it transfers a large, often the larger, part of what is taken from the consumer to the private pockets of the home producer.

I need not labour here a point which is so

clearly established. The important thing to grasp
is that of all methods of levying taxes so as to
reach incomes with a taxable capacity, tariffs are
the most wasteful and noxious in their direct and
indirect results.

Their worst result I have not yet mentioned. It
comes from interfering with the natural selection
which in each country tends to draw producing
power into the channels that are most productive
of wealth. That selection does not, it is true,
work with great exactitude. For the most profitable application of capital and labour from the
standpoint of a business entrepreneur is not
always its most productive application from the
national standpoint. But there is a tendency for
the profitable to coincide with the productive. A
tariff, however, is directed to encourage capital
and labour to flow away from more productive
trades into other trades which demand its aid precisely because they are less productive. The inevitable result is to lower the average productivity
of the whole supply of capital and labour, thus reducing the real income of the nation. Since the ultimate fund available by taxation for the public
revenue consists of the surplus of real wealth,
over and above what is needed to maintain the

capital and labour with some allowance for their future growth, it follows that a tariff, instead of adding to the public revenue, reduces it by reducing the fund from which alone it can be drawn.

§ 5. To this general exposure of the defects of a tariff may be added a few practical observations bearing upon the proposal to use it as a contribution to the special requirements of post-war finance. Foreign trade during the war has been so largely diverted from its ordinary channels as to afford no serviceable information as to the conditions likely to prevail when controls and other interferences are removed. In considering tariff revenue it will, therefore, be best to have recourse to the facts and figures of the last normal year, 1913, while allowing for some lasting alterations which the war will have produced.

The following Table gives the main divisions of our Import trade for 1913 in terms of money values:

IMPORTS INTO THE UNITED KINGDOM

Food, Drink and Tobacco:	Thousand £
From Foreign Countries	214,226
" British Possessions	75,975
	290,201

Raw Materials and Articles mainly manufac-
tured: Thousand £

  From Foreign Countries   190,283
  "   British Possessions 91,538

                                    281,821

Articles wholly or mainly manufactured:
  From Foreign Countries   170,257
  "   British Possessions 23,345

                                    193,602

Total Imports:
  From Foreign Countries   577,218
  "   British Possessions 191,515

                                    768,733

Now the Customs duties raised upon this 768
million pounds' worth of imports amounted in
1913 to a little over 35½ million pounds, a large
amount of which, viz., eleven millions, consisted
of food taxes which, as we have seen, are wholly
indefensible. This huge and ever-growing value
of total imports has played a large part in the
fond imagination of Protectionists, by appearing
to present an immense field of indirect taxation.
Before the war the political atmosphere was thick
with general tariffs, low at the food and raw
material base, and rising rapidly through the

successive stages towards a substantial tariff on fully manufactured goods. With this was commonly inserted a preference upon imports from our Empire, a concession which would not, however, seriously impair the yield of the tariff, seeing that the proportion of highly taxed manufactures of imperial origin would be very small.

§ 6. The war has had several effects upon this tariff policy, all detrimental to its yield for revenue purposes. In the first place, it will be impossible to advocate any new import duties upon either foods or raw materials, in view of the world shortage likely to exist for years to come. With this admission virtually disappears the substance of Imperial Preference. For nearly all the articles upon which substantial preference might be accorded are foods or raw materials, mostly articles of food already subjected to customs duties the detrimental character of which has been disclosed. There remains, therefore, only the third class of imports, described as 'Articles wholly or mainly manufactured,' and valued in 1910 at 194 million pounds. Supposing the foreigner (or the British consumer) could be made to pay a round average tax of 20 per cent., a tolerably high toll which would probably reduce considerably the importation and the yield of the duty, what would it amount to? A total of 39 millions, less the costs of collection, say, a net 37 millions. Before the war, in 1913, when the total national expenditure amounted to 198 milions, that might have operated as a sensible relief to the burden of direct taxation. But now that we are confronted with an expenditure of from three to four times the 1913 figure, the relief which such a customs revenue would give is almost negligible.

But the sum of 37 millions itself is only obtained by including under the taxable body of imports a large amount of articles which ought to be exempted as materials for British manufacturers. The following is the list of these materials extracted from the 1913 Table of articles classified as 'Wholly or mainly manufactured':

VALUE IN 1913.

	Thousand £
Blooms, billets, etc. . . . . . :	2,629
Copper, regular and precipitate . . .	1,449
Copper, old, fit only for manufacture . .	246
Copper, unwrought	7,346
Antimony, crude and regular	114
Lead, pig and sheet	3,718
Tin, in blocks and ingots	9,252
Zinc, crude	3,451
Metals, unwrought	1,679
Metals, old	567

	Thousand £
Cotton waste	516
Cochineal	85
Tanning substances	1,853
Dye woods	86
Gall	32
Leather	10,572
Oil seed-cake	2,540
Stones and slates	1,268
Cattle food	288
Pig iron	1,004
Puddled bars	7
Steel ingots	283
Platinum	381
Quicksilver	1,364

£50,730,000

If we remove this sum of 51 millions from the
total of 194, misnamed as 'wholly or mainly
manufactured,' we have only 143 million pounds'
worth of goods upon which the new tariff duties
could be improved. Our total revenue from this
source at a 20 per cent. tariff would only yield
29 millions, or, deducting costs of collection, a net
27 millions. If, as is probable, a preference were
given upon imperial imports of this class, some
reduction from this sum must be made. Allowing
for shrinkage of import value, owing to the operation of the new tax on goods accustomed hitherto

to a free market, the amount actually obtained by this reversal of our free-trade policy could hardly exceed 20 millions. As we have seen, a very small and an unreliable amount of this sum would be paid by the foreigner. Nearly all of it would eventually be drawn from consumers, *i.e.* producers' surplus-incomes in this country, diminishing the incomes accessible to direct taxation and causing a great deal of injurious friction in its shifting and its settlement.

PART II

CHAPTER I

OUR FINANCIAL EMERGENCY

§ 1. Having formulated the main principles of
sound taxation for the normal life of the modern
state, with the chief reforms in our present tax
system which the application of these principles
involve, we are confronted with the questions,
"How far are these principles and reforms adequate to the financial emergency in which Great
Britain stands after the war?" "Is it possible or
necessary to supplement normal methods of sound
finance by some special levy designed to relieve
the stress of the emergency and to expedite a
return to more normal conditions of finance?" In
order to furnish an answer to these questions, it
is necessary first to present an approximate
estimate of the financial situation when the
extraordinary expenditure involved in war has
been concluded. For this purpose, it will be
convenient to endeavour to forecast the situation
presented at the close of the year 1919-20 when

our national finance may be considered to have settled down on a more normal basis.

In round figures (it would be idle to aim at precision among so many incalculables) the situation at the close of the present financial year (1919-20) is likely to be this: The gross sum of the national debt will have risen from 650 millions, the pre-war figure, to at least 8000 millions. For the debt at the close of last financial year reached 7557 millions, and 275 millions is an exceedingly low estimate of the new borrowing needed to make both ends meet this year, when the estimated expenditure amounts to 1435 millions. For, making ample allowances for a large contribution from the sale of Government properties of various sorts, and for the maintenance of the excess-profits tax, or some equivalent, a large gap between revenue and expenditure admittedly exists, requiring increased borrowing.

Now, on the assumption that our Dominions make provision for the sums loaned to them, and deducting the pre-war interest on the pre-war debt, we are faced with the necessity of finding a war debt of 7000 millions. The interest on 7000 millions will be some 350 millions, to which must be added 35 millions for a low sinking fund at ½ per cent. Next year's pensions fund will admittedly exceed the 72 millions for this year, and may be placed at 80. This gives 465 millions as a direct war legacy. How large an addition must be made for the normal costs of military and civil government it is impossible to prognosticate, for these sums depend upon national policy. But, even if a peace be got so satisfactory and so well guaranteed as to secure the early withdrawal of all expeditionary forces and armies of occupation, it is impossible to expect that military, naval, and aerial expenditure can be reduced for some years to come to anything approaching the pre-war figures. The most sanguine of financiers could not hope to see the united expenditure upon these services down to a lower sum than 150 millions. It is equally certain that the civil expenditure must greatly exceed the pre-war level. Even were we to get rid entirely of the heavy subsidies for bread and railways, the higher level of prices, salaries, and wages for all materials and services, together with the new expenditure incurred on housing, education, land improvements, etc., must certainly involve an increase of purely civil expenditure from 95 millions in 1913-14 to at least double that sum. Indeed, a round estimate of 190 millions will be recognized by anyone who considers the circumstance an exceedingly conservative one.

But if we add to these sums, respectively 150 millions and 190 millions, to our estimates for debt and war pensions, viz., 465, we reach the total of 805, or, for convenience, say 800 millions. And even this makes no provision for many important tasks, such as improved transport, electrical development, etc., which will almost certainly demand large initial expenditure from the State.

§ 2. The early and considerable reduction of the war-debt therefore presents itself as a financial problem of immediate urgency. To its solution several proposals have been made in the nature of a levy upon the body of existing wealth or capital. If no such emergency step is possible, we are confronted by a situation which will oblige us to raise the income-tax and death-duties to a far higher level after the war than the highest point of war-taxation. For even if the lowered excess-profits duty, essentially a war tax, is retained, its yield must be very largely reduced, and the aggregate yield of tax-revenue from all present sources will show a very considerable deficit, even if a most conservative policy is pursued by the Government in regard to all new committals.

Now, is there any reasonable ground for anticipating that ordinary taxes will be more productive in 1920 than in the last year of war, when the total revenue from all sources amounted to 889 millions, towards which the excess profits-tax contributed 285 millions? Possibly customs and excise may furnish a few more millions. If the excess-profits tax were then entirely dropped, such elements of rising income as would have been brought under this tax would then become liable to income-tax and super-tax. Allow 20 millions for the former and 80 millions for the latter rise in ordinary tax-revenue, there will still remain a deficit of more than 100 millions.

Thus we shall be forced to face the alternative courses of raising the income-tax and death duties above the high level of war-time or reducing the size of the war debt by a special levy upon property. Another alternative, that of cutting down to a large extent civil and military expenditure, must be ruled out as impracticable. Though more careful administration of finance can make considerable reductions in the staffs and other costs of civil dependents, it cannot wholly stay that growth of expenditure demanded by increased efficiency of Government in every modern state. Nor is there any remarkable expectation that for some years to come the state of the world will be such as to bring about in this country a reduction of expenditure on armaments below the pre-war level.

Indeed, to place the deficit for 1920 at 100 millions is really an exceedingly conservative estimate. For it assumes that the artificially-swollen prices and money increases of war-time will be retained in peace-time, or will be compensated by enhanced productivity of industry and commerce on a not much reduced price basis. Now, though it is pretty certain that high incomes, so far as they are the natural expression of high prices, will remain, it is likely that there will be great difficulties in maintaining the full employment and the high productivity of war-time, for reasons in part financial and industrial, in part political. In assuming, therefore, that income-tax, and super-tax with the other minor contributions from customs and excise and other 'business' success, will remain at as high an aggregate as in the last year of war, I am taking a perhaps unduly favourable view of the revenue. But even so, there remains this deficit of 100 millions. If it had to be met by income-tax and death duties, contributing proportionately as now, some 95 millions more must be got from income and super-taxes. Since the yield of these taxes for 1918-19 was 290 millions, an increase of at least one-third would be required. In other words, the normal 6s. on unearned incomes would be raised to 8s.

Professor A. C. Pigou writing in the *Economic Journal* of June 1918, makes a more unfavourable computation of the post-war situation. He holds that the needed revenue after the war will amount to 800 millions (with no allowance for increased expenditure on the new social-economic policy), and, taking the 1917-18 basis of revenue from income- and super-tax estimates that "except so far as other duties are imposed—and broadly speaking other duties hamper and interfere with production more than the income-tax does—it would seem inevitable that income-tax and super-tax, which yielded £239 millions in 1917-18 will have to be raised permanently to double the rates which then ruled." The significance of this judgment is given in the following table which I may here adopt as approximating fairly closely to the situation expressed in my own computation based on the higher tax and revenue yield of the year 1918-19. If the 1917-18 rate of income-tax were doubled, so as to meet the requirements of the revenue,

Incomes of	£500	will pay	3/9	in the £	=	£93	leaving	£407
"	£1,000	"	5/-	"	=	£250	"	£750
"	£2,000	"	7/4	"	=	£733	"	£1,267
"	£5,500	"	8/8	"	=	£1,083	"	£1,417
"	£3,000	"	10/-	"	=	£1,500	"	£1,500
"	£5,000	"	11/3	"	=	£2,895	"	£2,125
"	£10,000	"	13/1	"	=	£6,541	"	£3,459
"	£30,000	"	15/8	"	=£23,500	"	£6,500
"	£75,000	"	16/2	"	=£60,624	"	£12,366
"	£100,000	"	16/7	"	=£82,916	"	£17,084

Now those who, examining this table, concentrate their attention upon the relatively large incomes remaining to the rich after the State has taken its increasing slice, may be disposed to approve this method of raising the required revenue, on general grounds of equality and utility. The £10,000 man can, they will say, easily afford the sacrifice of £6541, for the remainder will still enable him to live not merely in comfort but in luxury. Why should not the £100,000'er, whose swollen income is evidently the fruit of monopoly, give up nearly £83,000? The remaining £17,000 will satisfy all but his most extravagant tastes. At any rate, there is a double gain in attaching these high incomes. The revenue is benefited and productive power is diverted from luxury trades to useful employment by this reduced expenditure on superfluities.

But, while agreeing that the necessary revenue must be got out of the well-to-do with large ability

to pay, we must ask ourselves whether this is
the best and safest way of trying to get it. For,
if the attempt to get it were met by a refusal or
an inability to produce it, it would be best to try
another way. Now, there are reasons to believe
that some motives or incentives needed to bring
these high incomes within the reach of this taxation would be seriously impaired by so sudden and
large an increase of the graduated income-tax.
A raising of the income-tax normal rate from the
6s. level of 1918 to our 8s. level, or Professor
Pigou's 10s. level, would leave such a small proportion of the gain from the higher increments
of income to the recipients as to make it probable
that many of them would withhold the trouble of
earning them. Professor Pigou puts it thus:
"The extra effort which raises an income from
£2500 to £3000 would be mulcted of no less than
16s. 8d. in the £; that which raises one from
£9000 to £10,000 of 16s. 2d.; from £16,000 to
£20,000 of 16s. 11d.; from £30,000 to £40,000 of
17s.; from £75,000 to £100,000 of 17s. It seems
impossible to doubt that these tremendous rates—
tremendous even on additions to relatively low
incomes—must clearly check enterprise. The gain
left as a reward for success in risky undertakings
would be so small that many, who would otherwise

have ventured out of the beaten track, will no longer think it worth while to do so." Even if our reformed graduation were applied so as to reduce the taxable rate for the lower as compared with the higher incomes, the main difficulty would remain. Indeed a new difficulty would be added. For a graduated curve which should sensibly relieve the lower at the expense of the higher incomes would probably reach 20s. in the £ before the highest income level was tapped. Even my own proposed rate of 8s. would in a scientific graduation approach the same result in the highest incomes.

We need not overstress the difficulty. Some critics will deride the suggestion that any really productive effort is required from the recipients of these high surplus incomes. A landowner will take the highest ground rent his economic opportunities permit, even if 19s. in the £ of the rent were taken from him in taxation. So with the big proprietor or shareholder in business whose monopoly or quasi-monopoly enables them to earn great surplus profits. The 'effort' involved in earning the highest increments of this profit will be incurred not by the recipients of the surplus, but by the management and labour whose remuneration will be calculated to sustain this 'effort' and will not be 'mulcted' by the high taxation. Provided that the directorate and managerial staff have some real interest in making the business as profitable as possible, a very small share of surplus profits is required to furnish sufficient motives to the saving public to subscribe all the capital that is needed. To some considerable extent these considerations reduce the danger which Professor Pigou fears. Large incomes which are entirely unearned, in the sense that no productive effort, directorial, managerial, initiatory, or other, is put forth by the recipient in making them, cannot resist the highest demands of taxation. But, on the other hand, where even a moderate amount of exertion or sacrifice, or risk-taking, is involved in the earning of the higher increment of income, it is manifest that some reasonable proportion of that income must be secured as net personal gains to those called upon to exercise the effort, undergo the sacrifice, or incur the risk. It is not a question of ideal justice, or of the relative importance of the money to the private owner and the State. A great deal of the economic force which extorts very high payments from the consuming public from the goods or services it supplies is at the disposal of clear-headed business or professional men, who

plan and direct it into productive and socially useful channels. They can demand extraordinarily
high remuneration for this skilled initiative,
organization, and direction, which does involve the
expenditure of time, effort, and sometimes mental
drudgery. Though this rate of remuneration is
often grossly in excess of what they would be
willing to take, unless they received what they
would regard as a sufficient reward they would
not give their best care and judgment to the business. In a word, for such high increments of
income there must be a limit of taxability.

The same consideration is applicable to the
'sacrifice' of saving among those grades of savers
where the act of 'saving' is a conscious calculation
between present and future advantages. An
income-tax of 8s. or 10s. in the £, rising to come
17s. in its highest reaches, would undoubtedly
reduce the proportion of saving and investment
to spending. Though the portion of an income
that was spent would have to pay the same rate
of taxation as that which was saved, spending
would be stimulated and saving repressed. For,
while the full present enjoyment would be got
from the fixed portion that was spent, the future
enjoyment from the taxed income that was saved,
would be reduced by the further continuous taxa-

tion of the interest it earned. This consideration would have less force in restraint of savings on the higher incomes, in spite of the higher rate of taxation, than on the moderate incomes. For a very large proportion of the savings of the very rich is, as we have already recognized, an almost automatic accumulation of surplus income after a high habitual standard of personal expenditure has been provided. But for moderate incomes, subjected to higher taxation than has been customary, and with a smaller proportionate margin of surplus, the enhanced taxation will certainly diminish saving. The net effect, therefore, of a greatly raised income-tax upon certain important kinds of directorial and other mental productivity, and upon the proportion of saving to expenditure of private incomes, will be injurious. If this be so, the injurious effects will be exhibited in a reduced national productivity during subsequent years, or what amounts to the same thing, a reduced pace of industrial progress, with a damaging reaction upon the taxable body of wealth and the public revenue.

§ 3. The amount of such damage, however, is not gauged by these immediate reactions on the productive effort of our people. A raising of our income-tax to 8s. or 10s. would have other bad reactions upon our financial and commercial position in the world. The London money-market has hitherto been the place where most great enterprises all over the world have had their financial origin. That has been due to the fact that the quantity of capital there available for investment and for other financial operations has been so large as to attract to itself great resources from other rich countries for convenient and profitable handling in a common centre. The 'Bill on London,' the free market for gold, and the certainty of being able to raise large sums of money more cheaply and easily in London than elsewhere, laid a solid basis of financial confidence which has been exceedingly profitable not merely to our finance but to our foreign commerce and national industries. For a very large proportion of the loans and investments financed in London has gone out in the shape of export goods to foreign countries. Now any considerable rise in the taxation of interest upon capital raised in this country would strike a dangerous blow at this profitable business. For in order to induce foreign investors to subscribe to companies floated in London for railway development in Argentina or China, or for mining operations in Russia, it would be necessary to promise rates of interest far exceeding the highest pre-war limits, so as to secure to them even a moderate taxed return for their capital. Can it be doubted that under such circumstances the bulk of our financial business of this order would pass to New York where capital was available on easier terms, and that the stream of profitable commerce would follow the shift of financial supremacy? For America will be under no necessity to raise her income taxation to our level. Already she has opened effective competition for financial and commercial hegemony in South America and the Pacific, while her growing population and rapid manufacturing development force her to substitute to an ever-increasing extent manufactured goods for food and raw materials in her export trade. The high interest charges in this country, required to secure a minimum necessary return upon fresh invested capital, would so raise the cost of production and the level of prices for our manufactured goods in the markets of the world, as to make it exceedingly difficult, in competition with America, to pay for the imports necessary to feed our population, and furnish materials for our factories.

§ 4. To start our post-war industrial life with this crippling burden of nearly 400 millions taxation for interest and sinking fund upon the war

debt would be calamitous. Any sober business
man, confronted with such a situation in his own
affairs, would feel impelled to make the earliest
and fullest effort to reduce the burden of his
obligations and to restore his credit, even if he
had to sacrifice some of his sound holdings in
order to do so. A joint stock company or corporation, plunged into heavy indebtedness by some
unforseen emergency, would endeavor to induce
its shareholders to make an early effort to get
on to a sound financial basis again. Is a State,
regarded as an economic entity, relieved from
the obligation to follow this prudent course,
because the bulk of its debt is held by its own
citizens and involves a transaction by which
annual payments are collected from the body of
its taxpayers to be handed over to a more select
number of these taxpayers who are creditors? I
claim to have presented a *prima facie* case to the
contrary by indicating the dangers and difficulties
of collecting so great an annual sum through
the chief channel of our revenue, the income-
tax.

But it must not be forgotten that no inconsiderable part of our debt is held by foreigners.
Though no exact figures are available, financial
experts set the aggregate of our foreign borrow-

ing, inclusive of sales of foreign securities entrusted to our Government, at something like 1500 millions. This does not include the very large sums, withdrawn early in the war from financing foreign trade operations in various parts of the world and applied to finance the needs of our Government. Nor does it include the large sales of foreign securities effected by private owners in this country for conversion into money for subscriptions to war loans. The net effect of these financial operations will probably be to reduce our aggregate foreign holdings by something like 2000 millions and to create a positive indebtedness of another 1000 millions. Now this would signify a disturbance to our balance of foreign trade amounting to at least 150 millions per annum. In other words, if we are to maintain our necessary supplies of imported goods, we shall, by reason of our diminished interest on foreign investments and our new interest obligations on our foreign borrowings, be compelled to increase our export trade by at least 150 millions. And this we must do at a time when the world prices of the goods we import, foods and materials, will, by the circumstances of a world shortage, stand for years to come at a higher price level than the manufactures which we export.

It is true that, as we have shown, the selling price of our manufactured goods must, for internal trade at any rate, be raised by reason of this high rate of interest, and, we may add, the high money wages of labour. But for export trade, we shall have to sell at prices determined by the competition of countries less hampered than ourselves by these increases in cost. This necessity of 'dumping' our goods in foreign markets in order to pay for our necessary imports will be fraught with new risks to our people. For it will oblige all our exporting trades to organize themselves as strongly as possible so as to maintain the prices in the home market at a level high enough to support the dumping policy abroad. In order to do this, there would be a specious case for keeping out foreign manufactures from our markets. In other words, the establishment of tariff-protected and subsidized trusts, cartels and combines, would be an almost inevitable result of the financial and commercial pressures generated by the burden of war indebtedness.

§ 6. There is only one way of avoiding these perils, viz., by an early and drastic reduction of our national debt. The policy of debt redemption is admitted, and all State financiers propose some sinking fund for the purpose. But if this sinking

fund is operative in slow process over forty or
fifty years, the financial situation in the early
years of unsettlement following this war will be
fraught with all the perils I have described. The
only means of safety is the enlargement of this
sinking fund to such a size as to furnish immediate
or early relief. To establish a sinking fund which
would at once reduce the total indebtedness by
one-half, leaving the rest of the debt to the slower
process of redemption, would greatly ease the
situation. If, by a levy upon the capital wealth
of our people, we could reduce the debt now, or
at an early date, from 7000 millions to 3000
millions, the present rate of taxation might enable
the Government to meet its necessary expenses,
instead of being confronted with an annual deficit
of over 100 millions. For the reduction of interest
and sinking fund thus achieved would amount to
nearly 200 millions. This would seem to wipe
out the deficit, leaving some 100 millions surplus
in hand. The actual position, however, would not
be so favourable. For if this reduction of the debt
was achieved by a capital levy, the interest upon
the capital thus taken would no longer figure in
the annual income subject to taxation, while the
values passing each year as death duties would
also be reduced. Thus both sources of annual

revenue would suffer a reduction which must be taken into account in considering the net economy of the levy. The exact amount of the reduction cannot be estimated. For the latest official returns do not enable us to know what proportion of the yield of the income-tax is from rents and dividends and interest. Earlier Reports, however, give the yield for such unearned income at approximately three-fifths of the whole. Allowing for the heightened discrimination against unearned income in war-budgets, this proportion may reasonably be raised to two-thirds. Thus, according to the yield from unearned income, two-thirds of the net yield from income- and super-tax for 1918-19 (amounting to 290 millions), we should get a figure just below 194 millions. Next, taking the aggregate capital-values in this country susceptible to taxation at 16,500 millions (a figure from which we shall find a large amount of support), we perceive that a levy of 3,500,000,000 amounts to between one-fourth and one-fifth of the aggregate wealth. On this basis, the loss in yield of income-tax, on account of the capital levy, would be between 49 millions and 39 millions. Put it at 45 millions and add a proportionate amount of 4 or 5 millions for the reduced yield for death duties, and the

figure reached, say, 50 millions, would still leave
a small surplus in hand upon the basis of a retention of the present rate of income-tax. A levy of
some 3500 millions would, in a word, save us
from the dangerous alternative of raising in peace
time the rate of the war income-tax.

CHAPTER II

A LEVY ON WAR-MADE WEALTH

§ 1. There are two proposals for a levy upon
capital for the purpose of reducing the burden of
indebtedness which deserve consideration. The
first would confine the levy to the new capital
values created in the period of the war. The
general argument is to the effect that this increase
of wealth is presumably due in its origin to war
conditions, consisting in the main of squeezes and
wind-falls, the product of war needs and war
extravagances. Originating in this manner, much
of this enlarged capital has escaped taxation,
though the income it furnishes is taxed. It has
a large ability to pay, and a post-war levy made
upon it is in effect a correction of the financial
negligence and error which permitted this war-
made wealth to come into the possession of its

owner. It is contended that, at a time when war claimed from every one his proper sacrifices, such profits ought not to have been made, and that having been made, they ought to be reclaimed by the State, which could thus remedy in part the injuries caused by its loose war-finance.

The brunt of this contention is contained in its assertion of the magnitude of what is termed war-profiteering. Now, while it is common knowledge that great fortunes have been made during the war by various business firms and speculators, no close computation of the aggregate of such profiteering is available. If any special levy were to be placed upon it, the first step would necessarily be the appointment of a Commission, with authority to examine the accounts of businesses and individuals whose incomes showed a *prima facie* case for the existence of war-made capital, and to make a valuation of their pre-war and post-war properties, so as to ascertain the amount of this war-profiteering, with a view to its assessment for the special levy.

Over a great part of the business field no considerable difficulty would be encountered. For the large war-gains are for the most part registered in the increased value of the shares of public companies. The biggest profiteers are to be found in those trades which have passed through the stage of private businesses into that of joint stock companies with listed securities. The records of the war departments have already revealed a number of scandalous examples, and closer investigations made by a Commission with full powers to call for accounts would make further important disclosures. Now that almost all income-tax payers are required to disclose their incomes from all sources, it should be possible for the Income-Tax Commissioners, by the closer scrutiny needed for other purposes of tax reform, to give great assistance to the valuation of capital needed for the levy.

§ 2. As regards the aggregate quantity of such war-made wealth and the amount made by certain trades, we may cite certain facts and figures in order to establish a *prima facie* ground for supposing the quantity to be so large as to be capable of making a sensible reduction in the war-debt, if half of it could be recovered by a levy.

Before the war the annual aggregate savings of the nation were generally computed at some 400 millions available for investment at home or abroad. Sometimes they were put at the higher figure of 500 millions. About half of these savings were put into public Companies or Government or

Municipal loans, in this country or abroad. The other half were presumably absorbed in private business undertakings. Now the testimony furnished by the recent records of savings put into the former class of investments deserves attention. The subscriptions of 'New Capital' during recent years are as follows:—

1912	£210,850,000
1913	196,537,000
1914	512,522,600
1915	685,241,700
1916	585,436,400
1917	1,318,596,000
1918	1,393,381,400

These figures do not include Government borrowing in the form of Treasury Bills, nor do they take account of distributions of bonus shares. Now, though the great bulk of the national savings during war time has of course gone into war loans, there is no reason to doubt that as much money as usual has been 'put back into private businesses,' much of it indeed escaping taxation as income. When the quantity of outstanding Treasury Bills and other floating debt (some 1400 millions at. the close of the financial year) is taken into account, we have *prima facie* proof of new capital coming into existence during

the war amounting to a figure of not less than
6900 millions.[1] Allowing for the transfer of
money from the sale of foreign investments and
for contributions to our War Loans from
foreign sources, the amount of new savings
effected in this country during the war can
hardly be less than 5000 millions, exhibiting an
increase amounting to treble the pre-war rate.[2]
It is impossible to impute any large proportion of
this increased saving either to the undoubted
economy of the well-to-do classes in personal expenditure, or to the new savings of a considerable
section of the wage earners. It is certain that
several thousand millions of the money income
'saved' during the war, and mostly capitalized
in loans to the Government, represents swollen

WAR BORROWINGS AND NATIONAL DEBT
(*Statist*) *April* 5, 1919.

	War Loans.		National Debt.	
	April 1, 1918, to March 31, 1919.	Aug. 1, 1914, to March 31, 1919.	March 31, 1919.	March 31, 1918.
Floating Debt	1,557,522,000 223,324,000	5,785,798,000 1,395,610,000	6,240,729,000 1,411,971,000	4,683,207,000 1,188,647,000
Total..........1,780,846,000 Deduct Repay- ments......... 95,219,000	1,780,846,000 95,219,000	7,181,408,000 317,515,000	7,652,700,000 95,219,000	5,871,854,000 ....
Net Total.......1,685,627,000	1,685,627,000	6,863,893,000	7,557,481,000	5,871,854,000

August 1, 1914.......... 652,270,000

Increase since 1914...... 6,905,211,000

[2] 5000 millions is the figure adopted by Dr T. S. Stamp as the
net addition to individually owned capital during the war period.
See *Economic Journal,* June 1918.

profits obtained from business pulls or other advantages attributable to war conditions.

§ 3. Shipowners and shipbuilders, munition and other engineering works, mine-owners, contractors, controlled or free, supplying war stores of food, clothing, etc., to the Government, brewers, farmers, bankers, have made enormous gains, either directly from the high prices paid by the Government, or by squeezing the consumer under war conditions. To these must be added innumerable other minor profiteers taking advantage of war shortages to raise prices to extravagant heights on pretexts of dear materials and labour. Several reports of Government Committees reveal the huge profiteering done by many business firms in their dealings with the Government, especially with the Ministry of Munitions. But careful analysis, were it possible, would probably show that the biggest aggregate of profits were made by shipowners, brewers, farmers, and bankers. No published accounts give any true notion of their dimensions, which are concealed by various devices. The case of shipowners is particularly flagrant and has been brought before the public by statements of Sir Leo Chiozza Money,[1] whose official position as

---

[1] *The Herald*, Jan. 4; *cf.* also *The Times*.

a Secretary to the Ministry of Shipping gives authority to his revelation.

"In the first two years of the war the net profits of British shipowners came to about £300,000,000. In the same time the capital value of British ships rose by another £300,000,000." In respect to ships sunk by the enemy, Sir Leo informs us that "the Government paid out to shipowners the war price of ships," thus converting into cash these enormous war profits. It is important to realize that the bulk of the profits here indicated never figured as income and never contributed a penny to war taxation either under the head of income-tax or excess-profits tax. They were an addition to capital values attributable entirely to high freights and sinkings. These huge fortunes of shipowners came out of the misfortunes of war.

Bank profits are more obscure. They have been chiefly due to the extravagance and foolish borrowing policy of the Government. For the Government incited bankers to inflate the currency, by helping to create large volumes of credit, so that either by subscribing large sums themselves to war loans (*e.g.* the 200 millions furnished by the banks to the 1915 loan), or by advances to their customers or to insurance companies, enormous masses of sham-savings were concocted and handed over to the Government. The result of this inflation (supported by the Treasury's own 'printed money' in the shape of Treasury notes) was a rapid increase in prices, in money incomes and in bank deposits. Thus the banks made a double war-gain, first out of the dangerously enlarged credits given to support the war loans; secondly, out of the enlarged deposits thus brought into being and the high interest rates at which those enlarged resources could be loaned. The aggregate bank deposits at the end of 1918 were approximately twice the amount recorded at the end of 1913. Here again most of these war profits have been kept out of income, partly by putting them into reserves, partly by hiding them in an excessive writing down of securities, temporarily depreciated, which will recover value when it seems safe to realize them. The size of the war profits of the liquor trade in Great Britain as shown in the rise of capital value may be indicated by the following estimates for the first three years of the war. The "Brewers' Year Book for 1914" reckons the capital value of all breweries, distilleries, licensed houses, wines and spirit trades, etc., in the United Kingdom to amount to 240 millions. The Report of the Liquor Trade

Finance Committee, appointed in May 1917 to report on State Purchase and Control, put the
value of these same properties at the close of 1917
at the figure of 441 millions. Since that time
considerable further advances of value are indicated in the share market, in spite of the widely-
published statement of the recommendation of the
Committee that in the probable event of State
Purchase, the basis of valuation must be pre-war
profits.

The case of the landed interests, including
owners and tenant farmers, deserves a separate
word. The profits of all decently capable farmers
in most parts of the country have risen to unheard
of heights, as every country banker knows. From
the early rises there was no contribution to the
income-tax, which was fixed on a basis of assessing
profits at the ridiculously low figure of one-third
of the annual value. Even when in 1915, the basis
of assessment was raised to the full annual value,
the taxation was exceedingly low, the net yield for
1916-17 amounting to £2,850,000. Farmers' profits have been enhanced, not only by the fact of the
enormous rise of food prices, but by the legal pro-
hibition upon any rise of rent on sitting tenants
which prevented many landlords from taking most
of the increased profits in heightened rents, as

normally they could have done. But land-owners have by no means failed to participate in war prosperity. For all over the country they have been selling land, chiefly to their tenants, at prices based upon the inflated war prices and profits guaranteed by governmental subsidies. A large share of the farmers' war profits have thus passed to landowners in lump sums which, not ranking as income, are not subject to taxation, even the land values increment tax having been repealed in their favour.

§ 4. A great amount of other war-profiteering has also escaped the public eye and the income-tax by failing to figure as 'income' in any stage of its production. Where a firm doing war-work has been making extra high profits, it has, in many instances, been permitted to apply a very large proportion of these profits to the purpose of en-larging its plant and extending its business, in-stead of distributing it as dividend. This policy continued over several years, has enabled such fa-voured firms to convert income into capital and in-creased earning power, without paying any tax on such elements of income. The profit thus with-held from dividends, and reinvested in a business operating on a high profit level, will necessarily swell the size of the reserve until it reaches such

a magnitude that it is deemed well to capitalize
it in the form of 'bonus shares' allotted to existing shareholders either for no cash payment, or
for a payment less than their actual market value.
So far as the distribution of 'bonus shares' represents extra earnings withheld from distribution
as dividend at the time when they were earned,
it merely serves to conceal from the general eye
a part of the excess-profits upon which income-tax
is paid and to escape super-tax. But so far as the
bonus shares represent growth of capital value
due to further advances of price and profit rates,
and based upon estimates of high future earning
capacity, they constitute a distribution of unearned wealth which apparently does not rank
as income or contribute to taxation at any stage
either of its growth inside the reserve, or of its
distribution among the shareholders. Nor is this
growth of untaxed wealth confined to these cases.
It applies to all cases of enhancement of capital
values, such as have occurred in businesses fa-
voured by war conditions. I have cited the case
of shipping. Here was no instance merely of capitalizing reserves withheld from distribution as
dividends, but a continuous automatic growth of
values of ships due to freight conditions and governmental guarantees. These gains might be real-

ized by shareholders either in the shape of higher
dividends from existing shares, or in a distribution of bonus shares, or in a preferential right to
purchase new shares at a figure below their estimated market price. If the shareholders took
their gain in the first way, it would represent war
profit upon which income- or super-tax would be
incurred by them. But if they took their war gain
in bonus or new shares, they would incur no such
taxation upon the sum they received, but only on
the future interest paid on these new holdings.
The bonus or share distribution, when it is made,
ranks as an addition to their capital but not to
their income. And yet, if desired, it can be converted by the shareholder into cash, and used for
any purpose of expenditure. During the war immense increments of capital value have thus been
created and passed into the possession of the capitalist classes, contributing nothing to taxation,
even when they are realized in cash and spent.

This share distribution is, however, only one
of the ways in which this untaxed war gain is realized. Where no such distribution of capital increment takes place, the increased value of existing holdings, due to high present and prospective
dividends, may be converted into cash, and rank
as effective income to be spent, by any share-

holder who chooses to sell out. For the cash profit of such selling does not rank as taxable income, unless it is made in the regular way of business by a financier or professional speculator in some class of property.

Large masses of war-profits, unearned and untaxed, have within the past four years, thus passed into the possession of rich and fortunately-placed business men, to be retained in the business for the earning of high future dividends, to be invested in other lucrative businesses, to be loaned at 5 per cent. to the Government, or to be spent on objects of personal satisfaction. But the war-profiteering does not disappear with the war itself. This war has left the nation in possession of expensive and valuable properties in the shape of ships, factories, buildings, lands, machinery, vehicles and vast stores of materials of various kinds. Most of these properties have been bought by the nation during the war at profiteering prices. After the war they are being sold back, in many instances, to the very firms who supplied them to the Government, at prices far below their market value. The shipping, engineering and other war-profiteers are thus enabled to reap a second harvest as rich as the first. What they sold dear to the nation they buy back cheap from the nation.

This second harvest will be very gainful. For in few cases will the profit rank as income or excess-profits for purposes of taxation. Most of it will accrue to the purchasers as an addition to their capital. The shipping and engineering firms which buy the Government vessels and factories will pay no tax upon their profit from the deal.

§ 6. I have disclosed four principal forms of war-profits which have been incorporated in capital values without contributing to income- or super-tax or excess-profits tax in any appreciable degree. (1) The manufacture of credit by bankers and finance houses operating to inflate the currency and raise prices. (2) Extravagant prices, subventions and compensations paid by Government to private firms for goods, services or damage. (3) Extortionate prices exacted from consumers under the duress of war conditions. (4) Purchase from the Government after the war of plant, stocks, etc., at knock-out prices. The fact that income-tax, and, in the later war years, excess-profits tax, takes some considerable share of the increased annual income accruing from these dealings, does not dispose of the charge that war-gains, hitherto untaxed, have added several thousand million pounds to the property of the profiteers. That this mass of new wealth, due to war scarcity and risks, and obtained at the expense of the taxpayer or the consumer by a comparatively few rich, powerful, lucky or unscrupulous men, should have contributed little or nothing to the expenses of the war, is widely and justly resented, and lies at the root of our present discontents.

§ 7. It is no adequate answer to this criticism to urge that large quantities of capital values have depreciated under war conditions. Perhaps under an ideally equitable government compensation would be made for such war damage. But the taxation of positive income and increments has never been accompanied, in any State finance, by compensations for losses or decrements. The accepted attitude is that the State should raise its income from sources where there is ability to pay. Now here is a body of wealth which, considering its origins, its magnitude and its distribution, has a very high ability to pay. I speak of the capital wealth created by the war conditions, some of which will continue to accumulate for years to come. This body of wealth does not pay taxes. No doubt the annual income it yields to its holders pays income-tax, and the 'corpus' itself will eventually pay death duties. But neither of these payments meets our reasonable claim. If it be true that 300 millions has been added to the wealth of shipping companies by the war, an annual payment of the six or eight millions representing the income-tax upon the dividends of this enlarged capital is no adequate contribution to the revenue. Nor is it a reasonable ground for immunity, that in the course of the next thirty years it will all pay death duties. The critical situation of our finance requires that every source with a present capacity to pay should now be tapped.

No close computation of the aggregate amount of this war-profiteering is yet practicable. Much of it is not revealed in any published government or company accounts. Nor, as we see, is the process yet completed. Moreover, for the purpose of considering a levy on this wealth, some time must be allowed for the settlement of capital values.

The most authoritative conjecture of the increase of aggregate individual wealth during the war is that given by Dr J. C. Stamp,[1] who, after allowing for the depreciation of some values and the wholly incalculable character of others, registers this judgment: "These adjustments result in a net addition of £5250 millions to the individual wealth which would be both subject to, and likely to be revealed for the purposes of, a capital

[1] *Economic Journal*, Sept. 1918.

levy as generally put forward by its protagonists.'' In viewing this sum, however, as a measure of what we term war-profiteering reflected in
enhanced capital values, two considerations must
be taken into account. In the first place, Dr
Stamp is here concerned with measuring the total
increase of capital values during the war in connection with a proposal, not for a levy upon war-
made capital, but upon all forms of capital. He,
therefore, rightly deducts from his computation
of the increase such falls of value as have taken
place through our reduced holdings of foreign
investments, and the reduced value of railway
stocks. But, as we have already seen, any proposal to make a levy upon war-made capital alone,
upon the accumulated wealth due to war conditions, would not take account of these falls of
value except when they appeared as set offs
against war gain in the several businesses or ownerships assessed for the levy. Again, recognizing
that post-war values must depend largely upon
the rate of investment interest and the level of
prices, Dr Stamp assumes that while the former
will stay at the present 5 per cent. level, the latter will decline to an average level 25 per cent.
higher than before the war. In this latter assumption he will, however, find little support in any

business or financial quarter. Present prices are more than 100 per cent. above the pre-war level, and it is generally held that they will stand for a long time to come at 50 per cent. over that level.

Having regard, therefore, to these considerations, it would seem a reasonable assumption that the capitalized war gains which we are here investigating would amount to a considerably larger sum than 5250 millions. Some figure between 6000 millions and 7000 millions would seem not excessive. Nor would it ill accord with the knowledge we possess of the huge accumulations of wealth made during the war by many trades, firms, and individuals. Some 6000 millions will have been saved and invested in war-lendings, besides large sums subscribed to new issues of capital here and abroad, and still larger sums employed in extensions of business operations or put to reserves. While some 1600 millions of this saving and investments must rank as ordinary pre-war savings, and a considerable allowance may be made for an enlargement of this fund due to reduced personal expenditure among large sections of the rich and middle classes, the vast bulk of the increase of wealth is directly assignable to profiteering in the sense of taking advantage of war conditions to make and capitalize gains due to high prices and other favourable opportunities.

Would it not seem just and reasonable that this war-made capital should make a large contribution towards the reduction of the war debt? It has mostly originated in the extravagant expenditure and the bad finance which has been responsible for the unwieldy size of that debt. In other words, war debt largely represents war-profiteering. If our war-finance upon its revenue and expenditure sides had been conducted honestly and competently, most of this war debt would not have been incurred, the high prices which played into the hands of profiteers would not have occurred, and the new wealth which flowed into war loans and Treasury bills would not have been there to flow and would not have been wanted by the Government. The vicious circle made by war-debt and war-profits was due to the failure of the Government to finance the war out of taxation, supplemented by such borrowing as could be obtained by diverting into Government uses the enlarged amount of genuine savings which increased personal economy and the stoppage of unnecessary new issues of business capital would have supplied.

The *prima facie* case for assessing war-made

capital in order to repair the negligence and folly which led to its creation is, therefore, extremely strong. This ill-gotten gain, entirely the product of war destruction, war want and war extravagance, has contributed nothing to the cost of the war. Its income has made some contribution during the latter years of the war, the capital has made none. Why should not at least half this 6000 millions pounds or more be taken by a levy, either in a single lump sum, or if that be deemed dangerous or impracticable, in a quick series of instalments, so that the capital and interest of the war debt may be speedily reduced, and the otherwise inevitable increase of income-tax be avoided?

§ 8. Some readers will have observed that in this chapter the term war-profiteering is used in two or even three senses. Sometimes it is exclusively applied to abnormal and excessive gains made for war conditions and reflected in capital increase. At other times it is so applied as to cover all increased profits whether made from war-conditions or due mainly to other causes, such as improved methods of production or better business organization. Thirdly, it is sometimes used so as to cover all profits of any size or nature applied to the increase of capital. The full force of the plea for a levy on 'war-profiteering,' as expressed in increased wealth, is evidently applicable only to the first meaning. That some man should have made big money out of the war is a just cause of resentment, and a levy on this wealth appears a reasonable way of getting some of it back. To get all of it back would be impossible. For much of war-profits may have been spent by its recipients, not put to capital. But that seems no reason against getting back as much as possible of that which has remained in a capital form and is susceptible of a levy. Here, however, we encounter another difficulty, that of discriminating what we may call excessive and illegitimate war profit from that which is 'reasonable' and legitimate. For our analysis of ability to pay has required us for ordinary taxing purposes to recognize a reasonable and legitimate profit and a useful increase of capital. If we were to direct our levy, not exclusively to the excessive gains, but to all increases in capital during the war, we should appear to be neglecting this equitable distinction. Yet in any valuation that was attempted it might be impossible to reach any measured differentiation between the enlargements of capital that came from 'war-profiteering' in the vicious sense and those which represented the play of the normal forces of increase in profits and investments. All, I think, that could be done would be to exempt smaller proportionate increases of capital, and to apply a progressive levy upon larger ones, *i.e.* to presume that war-profiteering in the vicious sense varied directly with the proportion of the increase in capital values. This is the same sort of assumption adopted for the defence of the general equity and reasonability of a progressive income-tax, and it is applicable to the present case in, at least, an equal degree. For, though such a levy might hit hardly a few cases where enlarged capital value was primarily due to improved efficiency of method and organization and not to war conditions, there would be hardly any instances where war conditions had not contributed in an appreciable degree.

But there is a wider consideration, partly economic, partly ethical, which has, I think, a right bearing in favour of the imposition of a levy upon all new capital accumulated under war conditions, even including the savings that represent personal economy in expenditure. All such savings imply the acquisition during war time of wealth which is 'surplus,' in the sense that it is not needed for the maintenance of the owner's adequate standard of consumption. If a margin be allowed for small savings at such a time, it seems reason-

able and equitable that the nation should take for
the urgent national needs some share in all saving effected under the protection afforded by the
State, at a time when that protection has involved
unusual expenditure of life and money.

APPENDIX TO CHAPTER II

TAXATION OF WAR-MADE CAPITAL IN GERMANY

The *Reichsanzeiger* of Jan. 14 (1919) gives the Draft
of a proposed Levy on increases of capital value in
Germany during the period of the war.

The proposed law deals exclusively with individual
ownership, war profits made by Companies being taxed
in another way. According to the Draft, the difference
between the capital as determined on Dec. 31, 1913 (on
the occasion of the assessment for a supplementary tax
for defence purposes), and the capital to be determined
on Dec. 31, 1918, shall count as the taxable increase.
But, whereas the increase of capital from Dec. 31, 1913,
up to Dec. 31, 1916, has already been subjected to war
taxation, in accordance with the Tax Law of June 21,
1916, this special payment of war taxation is to be
treated as an advance payment towards the capital levy.

The chief provisions of the Law are as follows:—
These persons are liable

I. On the increase of their total taxable capital.
   (a) Subjects of the German Empire, excepting
       those resident abroad at least since Jan. 1,
       1914, with no domicile in the German Empire.

(*b*) Foreigners with a domicile, or habitually resident within the German Empire.

II. On the increase in their home industrial capital. All persons born in the country without regard to their nationality, domicile or abode.

The following are the more important deductions allowed from the capital assessed for the levy.

(1) Capital acquired "through legacy, life interest, entail or inherited property," as the result of a bequest, or otherwise from the estate of a deceased person. (2) The capital value of any charges upon the assets of the taxable person so far as, being restricted to the lifetime of a particular person, they may have ceased by his death during the period of assessment, so affecting the difference between the capital value in 1913 and 1918. (3) The amount of a capital payment in respect of insurance. (4) Capital acquired by gift or other transfer without 'consideration' during the period of assessment where the individual amounts of such gifts exceed Mk. 1000. (5) Capital, the proceeds of sale of foreign securities or other property non-taxable at the beginning of the period of assessment. (6) Capital representing payments as compensation for injuries made during period of assessment.

The 'ultimate capital' shall include the following:—

(1) Amounts given by the tax-payer during the assessment period as presents, or for regular payments of maintenance or education of anybody, pensions, charitable subscriptions, etc.

(2) Amounts invested in foreign industrial property during the period.

(3) Amounts expended on jewellery, *objets d'art et de luxe,* exceeding in the individual cases Mk. 500.

(4) Amounts expended on purchases of any kind during period of assessment, exceeding in the aggregate Mk. 10,000 (provided the articles are in the possession of the tax-payer at the end of the period).

CHAPTER III

A GENERAL LEVY UPON CAPITAL

§ 1. The 'levy upon capital' usually advocated, as for instance in the able book of Mr Pethick Lawrence,[1] is not, however, confined to war-made capital. The proposal is to wipe out the whole, or a large part, of the war debt by a levy, single or in several yearly instalments, upon the whole body of accumulated wealth in this country. It is urged on general grounds of equality of sacrifice and of 'ability to pay,' as the only adequate alternative to a crippling income-tax. A levy confined to war-made wealth would, it is argued, involve a double valuation, pre-war and post-war, very difficult to work, and could not easily or pos-

[1] "A Levy on Capital." Allen & Unwin.

sibly be made to yield an amount of revenue sufficient to wipe out enough of the debt. It may be
admitted that the latter objection is fatal to the
restricted levy, if it be insisted that the object of
the levy is the immediate or early extinction of the
debt and not its mere reduction to a level with
which the income-tax could cope. But, even if our
suggestion of a levy of 3500 millions, so as to wipe
out half the debt, were accepted, it is still arguable
that the basis of the levy should be the whole volume of the national capital, a process which would
utilize a wider 'ability to pay,' and would be
worked upon the simpler (though not too simple)
plan of a single post-war valuation. It might be
easier to gain the assent of the propertied and
ruling classes to a lighter levy on the larger sum,
and one capable of more graduation, than to a levy
of at least 50 per cent. upon those forms of wealth
alleged to be accumulated in war-time.

Accepting provisionally the conjecture of Dr
Stamp [1] that the amount of capital values susceptible of such a general levy is 16,000 millions, and
that one-fifth of this, could it be obtained by means
of such a levy, would enable us to wipe out half
the war-debt, we may best consider the feasibility
and advisability of such a measure by examining

[1] *Economic Journal*, June 1918.

the objections that are raised against the proposal. Some of them are economic, others ethical, and others relate to practical difficulties of assessment and collection.

§ 2. The economic and the ethical considerations are, however, related in that any feeling of injustice evoked by a levy may affect the springs of industry and saving, while practical difficulties connected with the valuation or collection or realization of the levy have important bearings on the economy of the process.

(1) Is there any inherent injustice in a levy? Is it a policy of plundering the rich? Does it involve a breach of the faith to subscribers to war loans? Is it repudiation? These charges have no foundation. A levy upon wealth in the form of capital is no more a plundering of the rich than is a tax upon the income of that capital. Were it confined, however, to the holders of war loans, it would violate the implicit understanding upon which the money was lent to the Government, and would *pro tanto* constitute repudiation. But, applied on equal terms to all accumulated wealth, it is not exposed to this interpretation.

It is simply an emergency application of the principle of ability to pay. Small amounts of capital would be exempt because, upon the one hand, they involve the largest quantity of real effort or sacrifice in their saving, while, on the other, the interest they earn is of the highest personal utility to the recipient and his family. The graduation of the levy, so as to take a proportion of the capital-value varying directly with the aggregate sum, is based upon the same principle of cost and utility as is seen to be applicable for taxation of income.

The general economic defence of the levy is that it is a matter of urgent national importance that the sum of the indebtedness shall be reduced at the earliest possible moment so as to avoid an injurious increase of the income-tax, and that the only means of doing this is an appropriation to this important public purpose of that portion of private accumulated wealth which is of least importance to its owners.

The policy and ethics of the proceedings are closely analogous to those of military conscription, in which the urgent need of the State is held to override the private rights which each competent citizen has in the vital resources of his personality. The substantial accuracy of this analogy is sometimes denied on the ground that it is not proposed to exempt from the levy the property of men who have been conscripted for mili-

tary services. But this is a casuistic evasion of
the real issue. In the grave national emergency
of the war the State calls upon the citizens to defend the nation by every resource which they can
contribute. Those who have both fighting and
financial capacity must contribute from both
sources: those who have only fighting capacity
must fight without paying: those who have only
paying capacity must pay without fighting. In
the great majority of cases direct personal service
must be afforded by the young who have accumulated little or no property to serve the national
cause. But where elderly men who are the chief
owners of property can also contribute personal
service, either to the fighting or the business conduct of the war, the State has just the same claim
upon their persons as upon their money. A really
monstrous wrong was done in financing the war
by high interest borrowings and insidious processes of inflation, instead of a direct application
of the conscription principle. The whole of the
loan money contributed in this country represented a surplus amount of income and capital
which could and should have been taken in taxation for the public need. To make an arrangement
by which wealthy persons, with large resources
available for assisting their country in its dire

need, were permitted to rack-rent the nation by a
rate of interest some 75 per cent. above the pre-
war level for the money they contributed to war
expenses, was a policy of cowardly folly. When,
as in modern warfare, it is the whole nation that
is at war, the obvious and equitable economy of
defence is that of conscripting all the necessary
fighting, working and paying resources, and of
putting the contributors on rations. It has been
admitted that war-work and war-bonds are as essential to the winning of the war as fighting, why
then this wasteful economy of high interest for
those who find the money, high wages for war-
workers, and a bare living allowance for those
who risk their lives?

§ 3. The main economic objection rests on an
insistence that nothing is gained to the State by
the seizure of capital that cannot equally well (or
better) be got by leaving the capital in its present
hands and taking whatever proportion of its present yield may be required, in the shape of income-
tax. For, it is argued, only the annual product
from the use of the capital, *i.e.* the income, is of
such a kind as to be available for meeting the current needs of public expenditure. If the State attaches the interest as it accrues, it is just as good
as attaching the capital. In fact, so runs the ar-

gument, it is better. For if the State assumes the
ownership of one-fifth of the capital of the country in the shape of land, houses, railways, mines,
factories and so forth, or liens upon the same,
it must either sell them in order to pay off the
debt, or keep and work them as national assets.
In the former case, it will cause a slump in the
values of these properties or shares by loading the
markets with them at a pace too rapid for absorp-
tion at previous prices. In the latter case, experience proves that the official management involved
by their retention will be less economical and otherwise less efficient than the private management
from which they have been taken.

Then follows an appeal to the ridiculous, in the
picture of a Treasury choked up with miscellaneous wealth in the shape of bills of sale, mortgages
upon estates, unmarketable shares, and even material wealth in the shape of pictures, jewellery
and bric-a-brac.

Now, leaving for consideration later on the serious question of valuation for a levy, I find very
little substance in this double contention that nothing is gained by substituting a single seizure of
capital for an annual seizure of its interest, and
that in fact a large part of the capital thus taken
would be in forms ill-adapted for the avowed pur-

pose of paying off the debt, or of accumulating sound assets to set against it. At first sight, regarded economically, it may appear to be a matter of indifference whether the State takes fifty or a hundred years to pay a debt (chiefly due to its own citizens, who have no power to make it bankrupt or distrain upon its assets), paying annual interest and small contributions to a sinking fund, or pays off the whole, or a large part, at once by means of a special levy upon funds possessing an ability to pay. But if it is a matter of grave urgency to reduce the debt at once, then a capital levy appears to be the only way of doing it. For, apart from the preliminary consideration of the positive danger of that increase of the income-tax which would be necessary in 1920 were no reduction of the debt possible, there are two strong financial arguments in favour of a levy. First, the borrowing effected under the pressure of immediate needs was at rates of interest reflecting this urgency, and the large volume of high-interest securities thus made has had two effects: first, to depress the value of earlier fixed-interest securities, and, secondly, to raise the general rate of interest for all newly-invested capital. Now the early extinction of a large proportion of the borrowing would necessarily reverse these two tendencies, helping to lower the rate of interest for new capital and raising the value of the depreciated securities. Both these effects are economically beneficent. For the high rate of interest, artificially created by war-borrowing, is detrimental to post-war restoration and expansion of industry and commerce, and is especially injurious to housing and other schemes of social improvement, whether carried out by private or by public enterprise. A reasonably high rate of interest may be desirable so as to evoke a large amount of saving and new capital, but the present rate would be so high as to depress the effective demand for capital (at any rate for home uses) more than to stimulate the supply of capital. Therefore, by paying off as soon as possible a large part of the war loans, the State would achieve an economy in production useful both for its own and the general needs. It would stimulate industrial and commercial enterprise and extend employment in a period when otherwise business men will be disposed, or obliged, to wait for an easier money market, with the result of causing grave risks of unemployment.

§ 4. Connected with this consideration is the special need for getting rid as soon as possible of two portions of the war-borrowing: first, the large floating debt in the shape of Treasury bills and other short-time obligations, and, secondly, the loans obtained from America and other foreign countries. The former is a shouting advertisement of the weak credit of a State which dare not fund its large floating debt, a weakness with damaging reactions both upon the market value of our funded debts, our future borrowing power, and, by a necessary implication, upon the soundness of our banking and other private financial institutions. The advisability of paying off as soon as possible the portion of the debt held outside the country is obvious.

Though no precise figures are yet available, it is generally held in financial quarters that during the war we have disposed of at least half of the 4000 foreign securities held in this country, and have, in addition, borrowed money abroad to the amount of perhaps 1000 millions. Against this no immediately available effort can be made on behalf of the sums loaned by us to our Allies and Dominions. This signifies that some 150 millions of our yearly imports, which formerly ranked as tribute from our foreign creditors, must either be dispensed with or must be paid for by increased exports of British goods at prices regulated by the necessity of finding foreign markets. Both of

these alternatives involve great difficulties and
hardships. To make so large a reduction of our
imports of foods or raw materials would cripple
alike our standard of consumption and our productivity. The reduced importation of partly
manufactured goods, or of wholly manufactured
goods, which are consumed in the productive processes of our industry and commerce, would have
the same injurious reaction upon national productivity. The quantity of imports which do not fall
within these categories forms a very small percentage of the whole. A certain quantity of foreign luxury goods, such as motor-cars, jewellery,
silks, wines and the like, might be excluded by a
prohibitive tariff, the effect of which would be to
stimulate in this country such of these luxury
trades as were technically feasible, drawing into
them capital and labour otherwise available for
more useful and important trades, and thus wors-
ening the net economy of the nation. The other
alternative, the extension of our export trade, so
as to meet our deficit on imports, though more
attractive, has difficulties of its own. If it involved
sending out greatly increased quantities of coal,
cotton and woollen goods, and other staple manufactures at prices which could force a largely increased world-market, it means a largely increased

productivity in our industries at a low cost of production. Now, however desirable this may seem as a theoretical solution, it can hardly be deemed practicable at a time when the workers of this country are everywhere demanding an increased share of the product and are in a disposition to enforce their demand, and when high wages, reduced hours, and dear materials and fuel are seriously affecting the cost of production in most of our large export trades. In time, it is true, new stimuli of efficiency may enable us so largely to raise our manufacturing productivity as to effect the needed expansion of exports. The natural and normal instrument for achieving a new balance of trade, whether by reduction of imports, expansion of exports, or both, would be the pressure of an adverse exchange. So long as £1 continues to be worth less and less in American dollars, a force is operative, reducing our ability to buy and pay for American goods, and stimulating Americans to buy our goods with their appreciated dollars. But this corrective force, having a large amount of compensation to achieve, will be slow in achieving it. The pressure on American firms to sell their surplus abroad and to build up national, or perhaps international, credit arrangements, so as to maintain the emergency export trade set up during the war, is likely to interfere seriously with the normal action of the machinery of exchange. Unless our statesmen are more than usually discreet and foresighted, they may easily be led into accepting further credit from America and landing this country deeper in debt. In any case, the remedy of rectifying a bad exchange would be so slow as to leave our financial position weak for some years to come and to leave behind a permanent damage to our financial primacy. An early release from our foreign indebtedness is, therefore, of urgent importance.

§ 5. Thirdly, it is clearly advantageous to release the State from as large a part of the burden as is possible while the artificially inflated prices and money incomes still obtain. Most of the war-lending has been provided out of the high money incomes derived from inflations of purchasing power and the soaring prices due to this and other war conditions. This meant that the man who in 1918 lent £100 to the Government at 5¼ per cent. lent only half the quantity of real wealth which that sum would have represented in 1913. If his debt remains unredeemed and, as is almost certain, the level of prices falls considerably during the years over which his loan extends, every fresh year's interest will put a larger quantity of pur-

chasing power into his hands, and the final redemption will give him back £100 worth a great
deal more than the £100 he originally lent. Apart
from this, there is the risk that, if the exceedingly
high income-tax which the annual payment for his
debt involves is long retained, a recurrence of
cyclical trade depression and greatly reduced
money income may put the finances of the country
into a dangerous embarrassment.

§ 6. There is one argument, however, urged by
Professor Scott in favour of a slow normal as compared with a sudden and immediate cancelment of
debt, which deserves attention. If we reverted
to the normal practice of paying interest with a
low sinking fund over a long term of years, the
burden could be gradually diminished by two processes; first, by a conversion of the debt when the
abnormally high rate of interest had come down;
secondly, by the normal growth of the yield of the
income-tax owing to the growing number of contributors and the general rise of incomes. Now, I
do not deny that, if we could get safely through the
finance of the next ten years, we might reach a
stage during which we could, availing ourselves of
both these alleviations, bear with comparative ease
the then diminishing burden of the war indebtedness. But the whole case for the levy rests upon

the post-war period of financial emergency. To tell a man struggling against a dangerous disease with a diminishing power of physical resistance, that if he lives, he will be as cheerful as ever next Christmas does not carry much conviction.

During the war, our Government has plunged into diseased finance which requires a drastic treatment for recovery. Opponents of a capital levy say that the remedy is worse than the disease, and that we should leave Nature to take its course. Here is the issue. Yet this analogy like others is apt to carry us too far. The issue between advocates and opponents of the levy is not so absolute. All are agreed that it is a good thing to pay off the debt. They differ as to the time-economy of the repayment and the method. The opponents of a capital levy would spread that repayment evenly over the next (say) fifty years out of the ordinary revenue; its advocates would effect a large early repayment out of an extraordinary revenue, leaving the subsequent smaller annual sums to be defrayed out of the ordinary revenue.

§ 7. Such a levy as is here proposed has, like most emergency measures, risks and difficulties of its own. It seems to some exceedingly unjust that material capital should pay the levy and that what is termed personal capital should not. A father

has two sons, to one of whom he gives £1000 to set
him up in business. With the use of this nest egg
he builds up a business which brings him in an income of £1000 a year, and has a capital value of
£10,000. The other son has £1000 expended on his
education, and with this advantage enters a profession in which his earning capacity is £1000 a
year. Why, it is asked, should the first son be
called upon to pay a levy of £100, while the latter
escapes scott free? Professor Pigou, in supporting a capital levy, is so harassed by this inequality
as to insist that the professional son should be
called upon to pay an extra income-tax in lieu of
the levy. There is, I think, no objection to this
course, provided that the rise thus imposed upon
the income-tax of professional men does not exceed their true ability to pay, either in the sense
of impairing their family standard of serviceable
expenditure, or of stimulating excessive and ultimately wasteful effort to enlarge their income so
as to meet the new charge upon it, or of reducing
their output of professional energy by reason of
the small proportion of the pay which it would
secure for them.

It must, however, be borne in mind that there
are good reasons against putting on the professional man an extra income-tax commensurate

with the capital levy on the business man. For, though the capital value of many businesses is largely dependent upon the personal capacity of their success, a large part of that value is usually vested in material forms, and the goodwill element of a well-established business as divorced from the personality of its manager is a considerable asset. The capitalized value of a normal professional income is much smaller than that of a normal business income yielding the same annual income, because the former is more dependent upon the skill, health, personal devotion, and other precarious conditions of an individual life. It would, therefore, be unreasonable to endeavour to get by means of enhanced income-tax from 'immaterial' capital an equivalent to the levy upon material capital.

Professor Scott seems to regard all tax discrimination in favour of earned as against unearned wealth as "obviously inequitable." "Many proposals for a levy are naïve attempts to shift the payment of the proportion of war costs which would otherwise be borne by earned incomes to the owners of material capital. This is obviously inequitable. If the war had been financed by raising the whole cost through taxation at the time, these incomes would have paid much higher income-tax and super-tax than the amounts which were actually demanded from them. By urging a capital levy they would free themselves from such proportion of taxes as they would have been liable to, if there had been no levy." [1] But why is it "obviously inequitable" to recognize the higher ability to pay which owners of unearned income or accumulated wealth possess? Our present income-tax recognizes it for the lower grades of income. Is the higher rate for unearned income "obviously inequitable"? Had the war been financed wholly out of current taxation, it would certainly have been necessary to have enlarged the differentiation between earned and unearned rates of taxation, for two good reasons. First, there is a reasonable presumption that unearned income is usually sup-plementary to earned income, and can, therefore, bear higher taxation more easily. If the effect of high taxation on unearned income is to stimulate the taxpayer to an increase of his lower-taxed earned income, so much the better from the indi-vidual and the social standpoint. Secondly, as we have seen, a very high tax on earned income is much more likely to curtail the output of produc-tive effort than a high tax on unearned income is to depress saving and investment. In other words, unearned wealth, whether as income or as capital,

[1] *Economic Journal*, Sept. 1918.

possesses a considerably larger 'ability to pay' than earned wealth. In attempting to supply the needs of revenue with the least injury to the tax-payer, and to the future productivity and revenue, it is equitable to take account of this distinction. Equality does not consist, as Professor Scott appears to think, in treating equally things that are not equal. In regard to taxable capacity £500 of earned income is not equal to £500 of unearned. If, as is contended, war-made and other capital possesses a real capacity to pay which has not been hitherto exploited, it is no valid objection to urge that the exploitation of this emergency source will relieve earned income from the obligation to pay a rate of taxation so high as to imperil the full use of earning power.[1]

When all these considerations are weighed, the proposal of an extra income-tax for 'personal capital' at a time when the ordinary income-tax must continue to be very high, will appear an expedient of doubtful value.

Moreover, it must be observed, that though equity in apportionment of taxes is very desirable, absolute equity will often be impracticable,

[1] My own rejection of discrimination between earned and un-earned incomes in a reformed income-tax is based upon practical difficulties, and not upon a denial of the distinction between ability to pay in earned or unearned income respectively.

and charges of unavoidable unfairness are not
fatal to a tax unless they are so grave as to en-
danger seriously the earning power of some class
of the community. I cannot think that this serious
danger attaches to a proposal to confine the capital levy to material capital and to exclude personal
capital both from this levy, and from an extra income-tax which under the special circumstances,
would be very burdensome and difficult to collect.

§ 8. Public revenue must be collected where it
can without too much difficulty be got. There will
be some sources with 'capacity to pay' that are
rightly ignored, if it is very difficult to trace,
assess, and collect them. If the sentiment of ab-
stract justice be offended in such cases, there is
no real remedy. But we may go further, and admit
that these inequalities will have some detrimental
influence upon personal and national economy.
Some persons are shocked at the proposal to make
a levy upon the accumulated income which thrifty
persons have saved and invested, and which has
contributed to the fighting of the war, or to the
future productivity of national industry, while the
income which unthrifty persons have extravagant-
ly spent on their personal pleasures escapes such
taxation altogether. They say with a certain
amount of truth that this course penalizes thrift

and industry. It was, indeed, to meet this objection that I suggested the possibility of a reduced income-tax upon smaller savings during a time like this when large quantities of new capital are needed. But this 'thrift' argument, if admitted, is liable to carry us too far. An industrious man who earns a considerable income has for his useful virtue to make a contribution to the State: an idle man who only works enough to provide himself with a bare living contributes nothing. Here is also a penalization of industry, or a premium on idleness. But what would you do? You cannot tax income which does not exist. Nor can you force 'civilized' men to produce taxable income in order that you may tax it, though there may be those prepared for this coercive policy which has often been applied to teach industry to 'niggers.'

I admit that, if you tax the fruits of industry and thrift too high, you impede and reduce the production of the taxable body. But I do not admit that a graduated emergency levy on capital will carry any appreciable danger of this sort. And that for two reasons. First, because the greater part of the wealth on which the heavier portion of the graduated levy falls is not to any sensible degree the product of a calculated and costly thrift, but the automatic overflow of incomes which exceed the standard of expenditure reckoned by their owners as desirable. A high levy upon this portion of accumulated wealth would not be an appreciable deterrent to accumulation. If, indeed, the combined taxation of income and of capital became a regular practice of our State, the aggregate volume of taxation might well prove injurious to production and accumulation, and might even cause industrial enterprise and its *entrepreneurs* to seek areas of lower taxation for their domicile. For this reason the advocates of a levy insist strongly on its emergency character, and the opponents on the apprehension of its repetition. If the State discovers that it can once 'raid' capital advantageously, will it not recur periodically to this method? The answer is 'No, not if you accredit it with any true regard to the economic interests of the nation, or even to the future interests of public revenue. It will not do so, precisely because of the soundness of the objection that is raised to such recurrence. And this recognition of the obvious folly of failing to distinguish between this unprecedented emergency and the ordinary needs of State finance will remove the apprehensions of future raids from operating on the minds of the saving classes so as to prevent them from saving. Of course, if one assumes that

State finance is going to be conducted in ordinary times in a recklessly shortsighted and incompetent way, with no regard to canons of ability to pay, or considerations of future revenue, the objection has validity. But in such discussions of finance as that on which we are engaged, we are entitled to assume a higher measure of competency and regard for the future than this objection implies. It is reasonable to regard this war-emergency as so exceptional and so severe that nothing resembling it is likely to recur in our time.

§ 9. The objection that a capital levy is likely to reduce the supply of business capital at a time when there is urgent need of large supplies rests partly on a simple fallacy, partly on the foregoing assumption that future saving will be checked by fears of another levy. The direct effect of a levy on the quantity of present capital available for financing new enterprise is nil. It is simply a book-keeping transaction by which certain sums will be taken from one set of capitalists to be paid over in cancelment of debt to another set—that is to say, so far as the levy is issued for paying off war-debt held within this country, as the great bulk is. The capital which is surrendered by the one set passes to the other set, or to the State, assuming that the latter chooses to hold certain parts of the levy (*e.g.* railway securities), instead of marketing them for the repayment of war-borrowing. The total amount of existing capital, real or monetary, available for promoting increased production of wealth, remains unaltered. Nor is it likely that its distribution will be very greatly affected, if we assume that all the well-to-do classes of our population have subscribed to war loans in a proportion roughly corresponding with their wealth. It is theoretically possible, no doubt, that the holders of war bonds paid off by the levy might spend the repaid loan, instead of re-investing it in business enterprises. But there is no ground for supposing them likely to take this course, unless we impute to them a most extravagant apprehension of another early levy. The capital levy, therefore, would not reduce the quantity of existing capital available for business purposes.

It is, however, sometimes suggested that though the present supply of real capital in the shape of plant, stocks, etc., would not be affected, the available supply of monetary capital might be reduced. A has £10,000 in war bonds which he has deposited at his bank as security for an overdraft of £8000. If £3000 of his war loan is taken and cancelled as his contribution to the levy, his bank advance will be correspondingly reduced. Since most business men utilize a large proportion of their war holdings for enlarging their bank credit, the levy for repayment of war debt may bring a considerable reduction of the bank credit otherwise available for re-establishing and enlarging productive enterprises. This objection has some force if it be assumed that pre-war banking business is to remain unchanged, and that the recently discovered powers of public credit are to remain unused, save for financial crisis, and are then to be applied only for the saving of private credit institutions from collapse. For the total volume of potential credit cannot be diminished by this reduction of private credit in repaying the public debt. What has happened is that the State has improved its credit by reduction of public indebtedness, and that this process has involved some (not, I think, a corresponding), reduction of the aggregate of bank-credit. The real wealth, the actual assets of the Nation, is not reduced, and so the aggregate of potential credit based on them is not reduced. But if the enlarged volume of State credit remained unrealized, the aggregate of actual credit, and so of power of industrial and commercial expansion, would certainly be diminished. This hypothesis, however, is hardly credible in view of the large experiments in the use of State credit during the war, and the large post-war capital-expenditure upon housing and other business proposals to which the Government is committed. The organization and use of State credit to supplement or to displace the private manufacture of credit by bankers must be recognized as a necessity of the near future and furnish a sufficient answer to the objection that the levy would reduce the available supply of monetary capital.

The further objection that a levy would detrimentally affect the future supply of savings has already been met by implication. It rests entirely on the assumption: (1) that a capital levy is, and will be regarded as an act of repudiation; (2) that it will evoke grave apprehensions of repeated recourse to the same 'raiding' method in the future. The first assumption is entirely false. A levy exclusively directed to war-borrowing would *pro tanto* amount to repudiation. But the contribution of war loan to a general levy does not, as is sometimes pretended, constitute a weaker form of repudiation. If any special discrimination were made either against the ownership of war loan or the income it yielded to its holders, the charge would be valid. But a levy which hits this kind of wealth equally with others is no more charge-

able with this offence than would be an increased
taxation upon all forms of unearned income without a corresponding increase upon earned income.
The second assumption, viz. that it will check
future saving through apprehension of further
raids rests, as I have shown, upon an imputation
of gross folly to our taxing authorities, and a complete failure on the part of all concerned to ap-
preciate the exceptional nature of the financial
emergency justifying this unprecedented step. My
contention is that capital has an ability to pay an
emergency levy, but not a corresponding ability to
pay a regular tax or a non-emergency levy, precisely because a general fear of a repetition of the
process would check the saving, damage production, and so reduce the yield of further taxation.
So far as any such apprehension is operative, I
agree that it militates against the policy of a levy.
But this apprehension I contend to be so feeble
that its operation cannot be taken as a serious off-
set against the advantages of a levy.

§ 10. I pass to the objection, also raised by Professor Scott, that ''The enforcement of a levy
could hardly fail to have a most prejudicial effect
on the position of London as an international
centre of exchange.'' ''There can be no little
doubt that a levy, in the circumstances indicated,

would produce a marked deterioration in the credit and reputation of London as an international money market, the effects of which would be felt for generations. Foreign capital that was in the habit of going to London would tend to be directed to New York or to other centres where there had been no levy." Would it? Why? No one proposes to levy upon foreign capital invested in this country. That will be quite safe. Why then should the credit of London suffer in the outside world? Professor Scott's contention here only assumes a general fear of raiding in the future, but ignores the grave results of the only alternative policy. I have already dwelt upon the menace to our exchange and our international financial position which a further large advance of income-tax involves. The danger from this, the sole alternative to a levy, is far more substantial than that which frightens Professor Scott. I am not, therefore, concerned to prove that *no* risk of this nature attaches to a levy, but only that a greater risk attaches to 'no levy.'

Finally, before quitting this part of the subject, I must express amazement at the charge that advocates of a levy are illogical if they do not stretch this levy to cover a complete repayment of the debt. Why is it illogical to use a levy as supplementary to high taxation which, if not thus aided, must become too high? A levy, as I have contended, is only an emergency method to reduce the value of indebtedness to a tolerable level and to ward off the early peril of having to meet the full interest and sinking fund demands out of ordinary current revenue at a time when industry is utterly unsettled and ordinary tax yields incalculable. The demand that a levy shall take all or more is but a shallow dialectical device for adding speciousness to the economic and ethical objections which are raised. The charge itself is utterly 'illogical.'

§ 11. But suppose that a levy is defensible in economic theory and in ethics, is it practicable? It seems to require, first, an early and reliable ascertainment and valuation of the various sorts of capital values; and, secondly, a collection in forms available for the purposes to which the levy is directed. Now, as regards valuation, the bulk of property exists in forms with a reliable monetary measure attached to them. Professor Pigou, in an estimate based upon returns for Estates Duty in 1913-14 and 1914-15, computes that some 60 per cent. of property at the end of the war will consist of stocks, funds, shares, etc., 4 per cent. of cash in home and bank, 4 per cent. in money on mortgage, etc., and 2 per cent. in policies on insurance. Thus 70 per cent. of the whole capital value should present no real difficulty for valuation. "Further, the most important of the other items, namely, house property, business premises and agricultural land" (16 per cent. of the whole) "could be roughly assessed on the basis of the income-tax returns, appeal being allowed to anyone who felt himself aggrieved." Trade assets, goodwills, etc., household goods, apparel and miscellaneous (largely personal) property (amounting to 10 per cent. as declared for estate duty, but probably underestimated these), present the real difficulty. Immediate official valuation for the purpose of early payment would not be practicable. But the adoption of Mr Sydney Arnold's proposal that the levy should be made on valuations made by owners and checked by subsequent official scrutiny, accompanied by heavy penalties for deliberate concealment or under valuation, would meet the difficulty, reducing evasion to a negligible minimum. It might, indeed, be well to recognize that some evasion will take place, partly in concealment of non-income-producing goods. It might be better to ignore this small percentage of wealth. The loss of yield would probably be less than that incurred by the failure of income-tax to reach the income which hides itself under additions to capital. Such escape, moreover, would not be final and complete, but would for the most part only mean deferred payment later on under death duties. The notion that, in order to avoid an impending levy, numbers of wealthy persons would buy diamonds and other valuables capable of easy concealment is fallacious. A few might take this course successfully, but, if many attempted it simultaneously, prices would rise heavily against them, and if, after the levy was over, they sought to convert their valuables again to cash, they would sustain a loss probably as great as the amount of the levy they had evaded. Something could doubtless be done in the way of concealment by buying bearer bonds, though it is likely that facility in evading income-tax and super-tax afforded by ownership of these securities has already had an effect in unduly raising their price. Any attempt on a large scale to use this as a way of avoiding an early levy would be attended by the same loss as in the case of valuables, the levy-dodger would lose both in the terms on which he bought and on the later terms on which he sold, and if he did not sell but held, in the low rate he would receive for his investment. In any case,

the leakage thus caused would be no greater for a
levy than for its alternative a higher income-tax.

§ 12. Could the levy be collected in forms available to secure its object, viz., the reduction of the
debt and the improvement of further credit? And
would not its collection absorb too much of the
fluid capital needed for the reorganization and extension of old businesses and the development of
new? In answer to the first question, it would be
both desirable and feasible to collect the great
bulk of the levy in cash or in war loan. This could
be done by offering slight premiums for payment
in these forms. Since most of the war loans must
be held by persons who will be called upon to pay
a levy, and the wealthy who will pay the bulk of
the graduated levy will be in most cases holders
of considerable blocks, there ought to be no difficulty in getting the greater part of a levy,
amounting to half the total war-loan issues, paid
in this paper, or in cash, and so available for immediate redemption. For the rest, the ingenious
proposal of Mr Arnold, that the Treasury should
issue a list of approved securities at certain fixed
quotations and exchange them with war stock
holders under an arrangement which offered the
latter a sufficient inducement to effect the exchange, offers a way out of a difficulty. "The list

would include Colonial Government Stocks, Indian Government Stocks, British Corporation Stocks, Loans of Public Bodies in the United Kingdom, Debentures and Prior Charges of the Home Railways, and of the best Colonial and Foreign Railways, and Debenture Stocks and Preference Shares of good Companies."[1] It might, however, not be necessary for the Treasury thus to dispose of these sound securities which the levy puts into its possession. It might continue to hold them as productive assets against the war-indebtedness, paying debt interest out of their annual yield. In certain cases, as with British Rails, and perhaps Mines, Banks and Insurance Companies, where an early policy of Nationalization was contemplated, it would clearly be advantageous to keep their securities for financing this operation, and even in other instances, where nationalization was not contemplated, a policy of tightening Government control in such matters as labour conditions, investment of capital, combinations and regulation of prices, might be facilitated by the retention of a large public interest in these enterprises. But, if the policy of getting rid of these securities at once, in order to apply the whole product of the levy to an immediate cancelment of debt, were pre-

[1] Mr Sydney Arnold, *The Economic Journal*, June 1918.

ferred, the process upon which Mr. Arnold relies, of procuring a voluntary exchange of these securities for war bonds, would, as he urges, present no difficulty at a time like this. Good irredeemable securities with fixed interest are better as a permanent holding than War Bonds, and there is a much greater prospect of their appreciating largely in capital value as time goes on, and as the high rate of interest upon new investments falls to which their temporary depreciation is due. If, as is possible, the sudden surrender of large quantities of war loans and gilt-edged securities injuriously weakened the credit facilities of business firms with the banks, the Government might take the course, already suggested, of bringing their own improved and largely unutilized credit into operation, either by way of guarantee to the banks or by direct dealing with this class of cases. Such cases, with others where the circumstances of ownership imposed peculiar hardships or damages upon the payment of a levy in serviceable forms, might well be referred to a Commission, empowered to substitute payment by instalments extending over a number of years. To such a Commission would likewise be referred hard cases, connected with trusts and other arrangements, where properties were loaded with obligations which reduced their real though not their legal ownership, and where a full levy would be inequitable. The difficulties, upon which so much stress is laid, connected with a levy upon real property and upon values locked up in the plant, stock, etc., of a private business, could mostly be solved by some such expedient. Spreading over the payment of the levy by a series of instalments would, of course, weaken the full efficiency of the levy. But it would not violate the principle which underlies it. That principle is that as much of the debt as is economically feasible should be paid off as soon as possible. If it can be shown that only a certain portion can conveniently be paid off immediately, but that another portion can be paid off by a fixed number of instalments extending over a few years, the rest being left to the action of the ordinary sources of revenue to defray the costs of a still slower sinking fund, it is right to recognize these limitations to the efficiency of a capital levy. But it is no argument against the use of the levy that it has these limitations. All I have contended is that, within such limitations, a powerful case can be made for incorporating such a levy in the financial policy which must be devised for dealing with the emergency created by the magnitude of the war indebtedness.

One word in conclusion. As in the case of the income-tax, small values should be exempted from a levy, and a careful graduation should be conducted so as to raise the rate proportionately with the size of the property. All economic, moral and practical considerations relating the ability to pay to the size of the taxable body are as applicable to a capital levy as to an income-tax, or ordinary death duties.

. . . . . .

In setting out the two forms of a capital levy, the one confined to wealth made during the war period, the other applicable to all accumulated wealth, and in discussing the advantages and difficulties of each form I have arrived at no conclusive judgment as to the form which may best be adopted in our financial emergency. A levy confined to war-made wealth would have the great advantage of a stronger and wider immediate appeal to the sense of justice which is outraged by the knowledge that great fortunes have been made out of the straits, the perils and the sufferings of our nation, and which would readily sanction the policy of reclaiming as much of this wealth as is attainable in order to apply it to the payment of war costs. A thoroughly sound war-finance would not have permitted this wealth to be amassed:

its recovery by means of a post-war levy is a correction of this error. Many who would boggle at accepting any general theory of surplus wealth in relation to ability to pay would be glad to take large chunks from the ill-gotten gains or windfalls of war-profiteers. Such a policy would also have a particularly soothing influence upon the mind of the working classes, dangerously suspicious of the connivance and support given to this war-profiteering by a 'capitalist government.' As a stroke of popular justice it would win general approval. But it is beset by two practical difficulties, one of which at least might prove insuperable. The ascertainment of war-profiteering as embodied in new capital values implies a fairly reliable valuation of pre-war capital in its several ownership. For the levy could not be levied merely upon a comparison of the pre-war and the post-war value of the several businesses, even if that often difficult computation could be made. For, as we have recognized, it is only individual income and property that have a true ability to pay. A comparison of the market price of share-capital in 1913 and 1919, or of dividends before and after the war, might afford some tolerably accurate measure of the war-made gains upon which it was desired to levy. But this basis could only

be equitable and practicable on the supposition
that the shares were held in 1919 by the same holders as in 1913, no sales having taken place by
means of which existing and prospective war-
profits were realized by the vendors. Moreover, a
1913 valuation might prove impossible in the case
of many private businesses, and, in any case, some
other instrument would have to be found for dealing with profitable businesses, not a few of which
have sprung up during the war itself. It is evident that this restricted levy could only be equitably worked by a comparison of individual wealth,
involving a 1913 valuation. Many persons hold
this retrospective valuation to be impossible. The
other objection is also of a practical nature. To
find so substantial a sum as 3500 millions from
this source would appear to demand a levy of no
less than 50 per cent. To recover this at a single
stroke from the men who have received it and
spent, invested, or even lost it, would in many
cases be impracticable, and an attempt to enforce
it would cause grave industrial and financial injuries to parties other than those immediately affected. Such a levy could only be executed in instalments which would extend over a good many
years. But this slow restriction of the levy would
defeat the main object of a levy, viz., to procure

a large immediate relief from the oppressive burden of the war debt.

If these objections are insuperable, the popular preference for the enforced levy must give place to the practical advantages of the general levy. Upon the critical issue of the practical possibility of a direct valuation of war-made wealth I do not pronounce. It is certain that a good deal of this wealth could not be traced or measured, *e.g.* the considerable gains made by many private shopkeepers and farmers. But it does not seem *prima facie* impossible that a strong, able, and impartial Committee (were such procurable), with Statutory powers to call for accounts and to summon witnesses, might trace large quantities of war-gains arising in certain fortunate trades and businesses to their real recipients and reclaim the bulk of them for the public revenue. The fact that other war-gains could not be so traced and taken ought not to bar recovery where it is possible. It is no valid answer to the recovery of certain stolen goods from the receivers that other stolen goods cannot be found. This analogy is no whit impaired by urging that in most cases no personal guilt attaches to those who in business have merely taken advantage of a strong situation in which the war has placed them. Wealth made by a combination of war-made shortages and extravagant public finance ought to belong to the public, and if it is stolen or lost in transit, it should be recovered where it can be found. In any case, the appointment of a Special Committee on War Profiteering, with a view to such recovery, ought, I think, to be made without delay. Before it is appointed, it may be premature to pronounce upon the impossibility of a restricted levy, capable of making a considerable yield to the redemption of the debt. The conviction of most of those who favour a levy is, however, opposed to the view that a sufficient sum of money could be got by such a levy, and they are firmly convinced that a general levy, involving a valuation of all accumulated wealth on its present value, is the only practicable alternative to a dangerously high income-tax.

CHAPTER IV

RELATIONS OF IMPERIAL TO LOCAL TAXATION

§ 1. Every modern State finds itself in need of a continually increasing income for the performance of new non-remunerative work, and for the enlargement and improvement of existing public ser-

vices. Comparatively little of this new or enlarged work is directly and specifically productive
of wealth upon which the cost of the State service
can be charged. Though public health, education,
defence and industrial regulations may be considered conducive to the improved economic productivity of the nation, this economic gain is not the
sole or even the main object of the State, nor is it
so certain, immediate and measurable as to furnish a specific revenue for the performance of the
public service, as in the case of the Post Office Services. The cost of most of these services must
therefore be defrayed out of the general income
of the State. That income must be obtained either
from the profitable exploitation of State properties and monopolies, or by general taxation.
Where, as in some countries, State ownership of
lands, forests, mines, railways, banks and other
lucrative resources, enables the public revenue
to be enriched by receiving rents and profits which
elsewhere are left in private hands, subsidies from
these sources may be applied to help to bear the
cost of non-remunerative services. But even in
these cases it appears that the rents and profits
thus taken by the State are in effect taxes upon
the income of citizens, in the shape of surcharges
on their purchase of the goods or services deliv-

ered to them by the State. For, when the State administers a productive and remunerative service of which it has a monopoly, it can either supply the goods or service at cost price to the community, or it can levy an arbitrary toll, working its public monopoly on business lines as would a private owner. If, in order to defray the cost of other specific services, or to improve the general revenue, the State pursues the latter policy, its action ought clearly to be recognized as a method of taxation. The determination of State policy is not, however, as a rule, guided by mere or immediate considerations of finance. Low railway rates may be given in order to promote health and amenities by helping to relieve the congestion of population in cities; a drink or tobacco monopoly may impose high prices and earn a high profit primarily for public order and hygiene or in order to check excessive consumption of luxuries. A well-administered State will certainly use its economic monopolies to achieve other serviceable objects than the provision of revenue. The desirability of providing cheap food, fuel, travel, carriage, insurance or credit, will, in many cases, disable the State from reaping a large direct revenue out of the economic services it owns or controls. To encourage or discourage certain habits of consumption may be deemed more truly profitable for a State, in relation both to its higher purposes and to the future economic productivity of the nation, than to exploit these monopolies for present purpose of maximum public revenue. Upon the whole, the tendency of a modern progressive State will be to use its increasing economic control to supply sound goods and services at cost price in all cases except where health, public order, or some other clearly defined advantage accrues from restricting or regulating the supply of the goods or services controlled. We cannot, therefore, hold it likely that our post-war State, however greatly it extends its ownership or control of specific industries or services, will utilize the power of monopoly thus obtained to any large extent as a source of public revenue. In other words, the great bulk of the increasing revenue the modern State demands must come out of ordinary taxation.

§ 2. Hence the demand for a thorough exploration of the taxability, or ability to pay, contained in the various elements of income possessed by members of the community. For all taxes, direct or indirect, upon whomsoever levied, are in the last resort deductions from the monetary and real incomes of individuals, transfers of their spending-power to the State. Death duties are taxes upon the parts of annual incomes which, not being spent, have accumulated, and can bear a second or special tax when they pass by death. Now those parts of income which are necessary to support the producers of that income in the output of their productive energy, have no taxable capacity. For any attempt to touch them would react in a reduction of the productive capacity of the nation, the source of the wealth from which all future taxes must be raised. Again, in a community where provision is made by individual saving for large increases in future production, in order to provide for the needs of an anticipated increase of population or a rising standard of consumption, a similar immunity from taxation must attach to the minimum interest necessary to evoke the required amount of that individual saving. The items of income needed to defray these costs of production have no true taxable capacity, and any tax which seeks or tends to assail them is *ipso facto* a bad tax. It follows that all surplus incomes over and above these costs possess taxable capacity in various degrees. Economic rents and all such portions of interest, profits, salaries, and other income as represent the operation of monopoly, scarcity, or some stroke of economic force or luck, some exploitation of a favourable opportunity, are the only proper objects of taxation. Not being due to any laborious effort or sacrifice on the part of their private recipient, their removal does not diminish his productivity, except in so far as their expenditure has been so embedded in a class or personal standard of living that a too sudden or violent attack upon it might cause an injurious failure to adapt himself at once to a lower standard. Apart from this consideration we find in these economic surpluses an absolute ability to pay. But the application to the practical problems of taxation of the distinction between costs with no capacity and surplus with absolute capacity to pay is full of difficulty. For, in the operations of industry and the emergence of personal income, it is seldom possible to distinguish accurately between costs and surplus, or to measure them. Even in the case of rents of land the part attributable to natural scarcity or situation or fertility is difficult to separate from the part attributable to improvements due to skill, enterprise and the investment of capital. In most other cases surplus is even more closely linked up with some legitimate payments for ability and saving. These considerations, though not invalidating the distinction between costs and surplus in respect to taxability, point to the inadvisability of basing any taxing-system upon the separate measurement of surplus elements in income. The practical basis of sound taxation is found in the presumption that the proportionate taxable capacity of individual incomes varies directly with their size, *i.e.* the larger the income, the larger the proportion of taxable surplus it contains.

§ 3. But the fact that the income, which in its acquisition is an individual income, is, in its expenditure, as a rule, a family income, has an important bearing upon the tax-policy. For it requires us, in considering the 'cost' part of an income, to take into account the size of the dependent family. Admitted already in the system of allowances for wife and other dependents, this principle must be fully incorporated in our taxing-policy so as to recognize that, as regards all low or moderate incomes, taxability varies inversely with the number of those dependent on the income. The income-tax, thus amended and graduated smoothly so as to avoid the irritation, injustice, and evasions, due to sudden jumps, curved more steeply on the higher grades in accordance with our general law of taxability, would remain the chief instrument for the collection of State revenue. It would be supplemented, as now, by the death duties, graduated still more steeply in the higher estates, by which would pass to the public purse large portions of surplus, accumulated sometimes through several generations, which had not been adequately tapped by any annual income-tax. A higher taxation of the larger annual incomes would, of course, in time slow down the accumulation of large estates, diminishing the proportionate, though not necessarily the absolute, contributions of death duties to the revenue.

§ 4. An intelligent interpretation of this taxing-policy condemns all taxes on commodities and other indirect taxation as vexatious and costly methods, injurious alike in their assessments and collection, their shifting and their incidence. Indirect taxes are occasionally defensible on other grounds than those of revenue, as instruments for checking the wasteful production and consumption of certain articles of luxury involving injury to health, morals or social order. Import duties, excise and licences, may be utilized for these purposes, bringing incidental revenue. But ordinary import duties, general or discriminative, are incapable of bringing any net gain to the national revenue. Ultimately falling upon the incomes of the people in the importing country, by raising prices and reducing the real value of their money incomes they inflict heavy damage. Costing much in expenses of collection, directing much of the capital and labour of the nation into less productive channels than they would otherwise have taken, and weakening the stimulus to the discovery and application of improved technique, they reduce the aggregate yield of wealth and so the 'surplus' from which State revenue can properly be derived. The rare cases in which the foreigner can be made to pay (*i.e.* when the import tax falls on foreign surplus incomes) are so precarious and incalculable as to make them rightly negligible in a taxing-policy. Import duties (unaccompanied by excise) are only defensible, if at all, for other purposes than revenue, for example, as a weapon in an international campaign against 'sweating.'

Such is the normal policy by which a progressive State should levy taxes, in order to supply itself with revenue. In order to meet the abnormal financial situation produced by the war, we have examined the practicability, economic and political, of two proposals for a capital levy, one of large dimensions confined in its incidence to capital values made during the war period, the other of a general kind, though of smaller dimensions. We came to the conclusion that, though it would not be practicable to add to the improved and more productive income-tax a capital levy as a normal or repeated instrument of revenue, these objections are overborne by the special considerations of the war-emergency. In other words, such a special levy as is here proposed would not have, the damaging reactions upon future savings, productivity and taxable yield which its opponents allege against it. Nor do the undoubted difficulties of valuation and collection precude its use.

.   .   .   .

§ 5. To this general summary of the theory and policy of taxation I desire to add the following important implication. If this policy be consistently adopted and developed as the instrument for State revenue, the long delayed adjustment between national and local finance becomes extremely urgent.

The services financed by local government may be conveniently grouped under two heads. First come those productive enterprises such as supply water, gas, and electricity, tram service, etc., to private citizens, for which specific payments are made by them either in the shape of a separate rate or by retail payments for each unit of supply. These are ordinary business transactions with which imperial finance has no proper connexion.

except so far as the State may be required to sanction the raising of loans for capital expenditure. The revenue thus raised is not tax revenue. Attempts have frequently been made in theory and in practice to distinguish among the numerous other services locally administered certain ones as being of distinctively national value from others of merely or mainly local value. Among the former are commonly placed such services as Education, Public Health, and Poor Relief; among the latter such material arrangements and improvements as the making and repair of streets, their cleaning and lighting, and the provision of parks, libraries, museums, etc. But a little reflection shows that the alleged distinction between services of national and services of local benefit cannot be maintained. In all alike the primary benefit is confined to the local inhabitants: in all these local benefits alike the nation participates. For in modern times there is nowhere to be found such municipal self-sufficiency as prevailed in the medieval city, and survived in some measure up to railway days. Commerce, communications, mobility of population have conspired to destroy the old localism.

We cannot therefore deal with municipal finance by merely asking and answering the question *cui*

bono? For local and national benefits interpene-
trate and are indistinguishable. And yet it is undeniable that the citizens of Birmingham or Brad-
ford have a far keener and stronger interest in
their streets or trams, or schools, than has the rest
of the nation, and that in virtue of this special interest there devolves in them an important or even
a predominant part in their administration and
finance. Evidently the chief direct control of their
paving, lighting, care of local poor, must be vested
in the local authorities, who alone can know the
detailed circumstances. But it is equally evident
that the wider national interest carries a duty of
supervisory control, and that these two controls
must both be represented in finance. The municipality cannot be allowed to determine or to ad-
minister an expensive policy for which it has no
financial responsibility. It is equally clear that,
if the State is to require conformity to a national
standard of efficiency on the part of local administrators, it must be prepared to assist in the
finance. With the development of the national
standard this policy of national supervision, ad-
vice, and finances must continually assume greater
prominence, and an increasing part of the required expenditure will devolve upon the State.
This consideration gives great importance to the

invention of the Grant in Aid as the instrument of national and local corporation in municipal services. Mr Sidney Webb has given the following account of the objects which this invention is designed to serve.

"Grants in Aid are necessary, in the first case, to prevent an extreme inequality of burden between one district and another. To leave each Local Authority to pay for its own sanitation, its own schools, its own roads and bridges, its own sick and infirm and its own aged poor, would mean that some districts would have to incur a rate in the pound ten or even twenty times as great as others." But the achievement of the object depends, as Mr Webb shows, upon the proper allocation of Grants in Aid. "The way actually to aggravate this inequality, and to transform the Grant in Aid from a beneficent to a maleficent force is to make it vary in proportion to the rateable value of each district, which is actually how several of the Grants in Aid have been allocated, thus giving to the richer districts which have least administration to pay for, and the greatest means, more than to the poorer districts, which have most administration to pay for and the least means."[1]

The second object achievable by Grants in Aid

[1] "Grants in Aid," ch. ii. (Longmans.)

is that ''They are needed to give weight to the suggestions, criticism and authoritative instructions by which the Central Authority seeks to secure greater efficiency and economy of administration.'' Thirdly, ''They furnish the only practicable method, consistent with local autonomy, of bringing to bear upon local administration the wisdom of experience, superiority of knowledge, and breadth of view which, as compared with the administrators of any small town, a central executive department cannot fail to acquire, for the carrying into effect the general policy which Parliament has prescribed.'' ''The fourth reason for Grants in Aid is that only by this means can we hope to enforce on all Local Authorities that 'National Minimum' of efficiency in local services which we now see to be indispensable in the national interest.''

§ 6. The funds contributed by the State as Grants in Aid to local services must, of course, in accordance with the analysis of the incidence of national taxation adopted here be derived from the general body of surplus or taxable income. But what is the fund upon which Local Authorities can properly draw for their contribution to the maintenance of local services for which specific payments are not taken? Do the local benefits de-

rived from these services take a definitely economic shape in measurable terms of improved
income for any class of citizens? If they do, then
there emerges a body of wealth due to public expenditure upon which a rate may equitably and
economically be levied to defray that expenditure
in whole or part. Now it is certain that clean, well
paved, and well lighted streets, open spaces, and
other local utilities and amenities, helping to draw
into the town some population from the country,
or from neighbouring, but worse-equipped towns,
increase the ground value and the annual rental
which landowners can claim. Is this the only taxable surplus created by public expenditure upon
these utilities and amenities? Some say yes, argu-
ing that any other benefits, whether economic or
not, which such public services render to business
and professional men and to private residents, are
charged up against these primary beneficiaries in
higher rents. Though house-owners or lease-own-
ers, as distinct from ground landlords, will get
some gain out of the situation, the whole advantage will, they urge, eventually pass into the
pockets of the landowners. Shopkeepers may
begin to benefit because the town made healthy and
agreeable by the public policy, has drawn well-to-
do residents. But shop rents will soon go up, the

owners of the property taking the gain. So with the advantage which the general growth of population and of demand will bring to other business and professional men, it will in every case enable the landlord to raise his rent.

But this extreme position attributed to landowners by many single-taxers is not seriously tenable. It rests on the assumption that the local land is strictly limited in amount, and belongs to a single landowner, and that business men and residents have no option of transferring their business and homes to other local areas. Now this assumption is invalid. Even in the case when all the town area is owned by one man, his power to take by rack-renting the whole economic benefits of municipal expenditure is limited by several considerations. The first and most obvious, of course, is the existence of leases which secure to tenants during the remainder of their tenancy the whole or part of the economic benefits. But apart from this, the monopoly of town land is qualified by the policy of most municipalities in enlarging the effective town area, for residential and for many business purposes, by cheap and rapid transport to outside belts of land, often accompanied by enlargement of the municipal area. This increased supply of land accompanied by development of building sites in suburban areas can operate as an effective restraint upon the raising of rents either by ground landlords or lessors of town buildings. This power of businesses to go outside the town area is an important and growing check upon town landlords, which may be made extremely effective when not only cheap transport but cheap electric power for industrial uses is obtainable. Further, although the inconvenience and loss incurred by moving a place of business or a residence from one town to another, or even from one part of the same town to another part, is a real source of economic strength to landlords, the existence of other neighbouring towns, pursuing a similar progressive policy of municipal development, furnishes a powerful element of competition for persons not tied down closely to a single central town area. These are real checks upon the power of a monopolist landlord to secure for himself the full economic value of municipal improvements. While, then, it is undeniable that a large part of such gains from monopoly expenditure fall to the landowner and lease-holders (during the period of the lease) it is equally the case that industrialists, tradesmen, professional men, and other occupants, are partakers to a considerable extent of these gains. So far as the benefits from such municipal expenditure are non-economic gains, such as health, intelligence, and recreation, they produce no fund capable of bearing a rate. But when the benefits accrue in real and monetary income, there is clearly a valid case for rating this income, so far as it can be ascertained or reasonably presumed, for the support of the local expenditure to which it owes its origin.

§ 7. The existing rating system which confines its demands to income from real property, land and its 'improvements,' can only be defended, on the ground that other municipally made income is too elusive to reach although it certainly exists and has ability to pay. It cannot seriously be maintained that the rental of business premises or a house is any reliable index of the possession of these economic gains from municipal expenditure on the part of the occupier. There is no complete solution of the problem of how to secure for locally administrative services the economic surpluses created by those services. For, as we recognize, in no respect is a town or other local unit so compact and separate an economic area that outside factors do not enter into every aspect of its economic life. Though an increase of town land values is evidently due in part to local expenditure in its influence upon the population and prosperity of the town, these very elements of population and prosperity are largely affected by other general outside factors which may be termed national, and which in their turn are influenced by still wider tendencies. Still more is this true of benefits which accrue to other citizens from the civic expenditure. Traders, professional men and workers in a progressive well-administered city will all enjoy certain advantages realized in concrete terms of real income or increased earning power. Part is due to the local good government. But how much it is impossible to gauge.

A revised taxing-system must have regard to these difficulties. It will, I think, do well to discriminate between the increases of land values due to local administration and other economic gains. So large a part do local improvements play in the former case as to justify a special contribution from this source. This could take shape in a special local tax on land values so assessed as to stimulate landowners to put their land to its most productive use. Since, however, it cannot be presumed that land values or even their annual increments are wholly or even chiefly attributable to local expenditure, the interest of the State in this form of surplus value must be duly safeguarded by a strict limitation of this rating power upon land values.

On the other hand, it is clearly desirable that Local Authorities should have incomes at their own disposal, derived from local sources, and put to local beneficial uses. A local income-tax, or a sur-tax on local incomes, sometimes suggested, is quite impracticable. If such a tax were confined to persons residing in the local area, evidently many of the richest business people would escape, having their domicile outside. Moreover, an increasing number of the larger and more lucrative businesses are not confined within one local area, either for their operation or their market, and in such cases it would be impossible to earmark any proportion of the income as earned in one locality. How could a railway, a bank, a branch shop, or even a local firm of lawyers, stock brokers or dealers, be assessed for income earned within any single municipal area? There is clearly no such relation between an income area and an area of local administration as to give validity to any such proposal.

§ 8. What is required is some approximately sound way of getting a special contribution to local expenditure from persons whose incomes presumably contain elements due to such expenditure. Since this cannot be achieved by a residential income-tax, some other index of ability to pay must be recognized. The present basis of annual rental value of occupied buildings appears to me to be the best available index, provided certain important changes in assessment are made. In the first place, since it is locally made income we are seeking to tap, the same process of graduation as is applied for imperial income-tax is applicable here. The failure to carry even the slight and clumsy graduation adopted for rentals below £100 beyond that limit is a quite indefensible application of the taxing principle. But if housing accommodation is to be taken as an index of locally created income, the rating must have regard also to the general test of ability to bear furnished by the number of persons dependent on the housing accommodation. A ten-room house occupied by a family of nine must not be rated on the same terms as if the occupants were only three. The rating in the two cases need not be in the ratio of 3 to 1, for a large proportion of the accommodation of a house has small reference to the number of its occupants. Nor is it desirable to apply inducements to overcrowding or even to excessive economy on house room. But a considerable allowance in the rating system for number of occupants ought to be made.

If, as is sometimes pleaded, certain persons choose to spend a larger proportion of their income than others on a large showy house in an expensive neighbourhood they will doubtless be disproportionately rated. But this is a doubly serviceable result. For by operating as a deterrent against extravagant expenditure on housing, it economizes for the general body of citizens the aggregate supply of housing and tends to lower rents. Finally, if a sound and equitable rating is to be effected, the methods of assessment must be improved. This can only be achieved by entrusting the process of valuation to properly trained persons appointed by the Local Government Board, instead of to officials appointed by Local Authorities notoriously influenced in rating cases by personal interest. It is well-known that the assessment by Local Authorities, especially in rural districts, is often incompetent, slovenly and dishonest. The under-assessment of large properties belonging to members of the taxing authority, their friends and other persons of local influence, involving a higher general rate than should be necessary, is a frequent and notorious scandal.

If it were possible to discover and to measure

with moderate accuracy the pecuniary gains derived by private citizens and local businesses from local services, it would be convenient and equitable to defray the cost of such services entirely by means of rates laid upon this publicly created surplus. But as a municipality or other local area tends to become less and less a self-sufficing unit for all economic and other purposes, it must become continually less possible to track down and measure such locally made gains. For this reason it will be necessary for the State continually to exercise a more rigorous supervision of local rating, so as to restrain the Local Authority from trenching upon taxable resources which are not properly local surpluses and which are needed for imperial purposes. This restriction will probably be accompanied by an increasing dependence upon Grants in Aid for important local services. This, however, need not be taken as self-evident. For just as a valid internationalism requires and stimulates distinctive qualities and capacities in its national constituents, so a valid nationalism should not aim at a too rigid standardization of local conditions, but should encourage local character to express itself in institutions and services administered and financed mainly or entirely from local resources. The art of municipal self-govern-

ment is still immature and experimental, and
financial policy should make allowance for freedom of growth, and for the utilization of the
keener public spirit which breathes within the
smaller areas of human fellowship. While, therefore, it is likely and reasonable that State control
and State finance will figure more largely in certain spheres of local government, this is quite consistent with a wider local autonomy in other
spheres, the larger aggregate of civic services af-
fording scope for both tendencies. So intimately
are the secret springs of economic prosperity associated with all services which constitute to human health, development, and happiness that it
may be taken as a sound assumption that, though
these services may be directed primarily to the
attainment of non-economic objects, the higher
standard of personal and collective humanity
which they establish will yield as a necessary by-
product such increase of wealth as will serve to
defray the public expenditure those services involve, local equally with national. Such increments are in accordance with our general theory
of taxation naturally adapted and designed for
this public purpose.

§ 9. This brief consideration of the relations between Central and Local Government, in respect

of the raising of revenue for public services, greatly strengthens the acceptance of our basic principle that taxing authorities find in surplus incomes the only funds with true ability to pay. Where there is a legitimate presumption that certain of these surplus values are directly traceable to benefits accruing from local public expenditure there is a strong *prima facie* ground for earmarking such values for contribution to the local revenue. Here is the case alike for local taxation of increments of land values within the locality and for a reformed general rating upon the present occupation basis. But the impossibility of ascribing any element of surplus income wholly to local public benefit, as distinguished from the operations of national policy or of *private* economic needs and opportunities, makes it improper for any local administration to rely wholly on its own rating powers for its income. For this would involve a continual danger of the locality poaching upon the legitimate resources of the State, the Local competing with the Central Government in its demands upon the same body of taxable wealth. Upon all surplus-income, except such as is presumably due to locally financed services, the State has a rightful lien for taxing purposes out of which to defray such costs of National Government as cannot conveniently be met from State-owned properties and monopolies, including under the term National Government such control of and participation in locally administered services as it helps to support by contributions from the national treasury in the shape of Loans, Subsidies or Grants in Aid.

INDEX

Ability to pay, 3, 107, 191, 206, 208, 231, 248
Agricultural profits, 101, 102, 173
Alcohol, 59, 122
Allowance system, 77
America, 198; income taxation, 159
American goods, 200
Arnold, Sydney, 218, 220

Bank accounts, 109
Bank deposits, 172
Bank profits, 171
Big business, 97
Bonus shares, 175
Bonuses, 111
Bread tax, 55
Breakfast duties, 122
Building operations, 32
Business ability, 24

Capital, business, 211; deduction for levy, German, 188; fresh, 68, 71; land values and, 80; material vs. personal, 203-204; minimum rate of interest, 18; new, 168; private, 72; see also Levy on capital
Capitalistic government, 225
Cartels, 128
Cinemas, 57
Clothing, 57
Cocoa, 122
Coffee, 122
Collection, 220, 236; at the source, 105, 107
Combination, 35, 36
Comfort, standards of, 17
Commodities, 47, 235; incidence and shifting of tax on, 54
Competition, 35
Conscription, 192
Consumer, insensitiveness, 65; making him pay the tax, 49; shifting the tax, 52; ultimate, 136
Cost of production, 16; profits, minority of, 21; standard wage as an element, 17
Costs, surplus distinguished from, 26, 45, 67; taxation of, 44
Credit, 213
Current income, 10
Customs duties, 122
Cutting the melon, 111

Death duties, 7-8, 10, 110, 232
Debt, national, 146; See also War debt
Direct taxation, 8, 64, 104
Discontent, root of, 179
Discrimination, 98, 205
Dumping, 129, 162

Earned and unearned incomes, 95, 205
Economic monopoly, 30
Education, 71, 73
Emergency, financial, 145, 210, 211
Encroachment, 72, 104
Endowment policies, 101
Entrepreneur, 23
Evasion, 218
Excess-profits taxation, 69
Exchange, 200
Exemptions, 77
Export trade, 162, 199

Family as unit of expenditure, 88

Family income, 86

Farmers. *See* Agricultural profits

Finance, central problem of new state, 38; new moral basis, 78; war, 203

Financial emergency, 145, 210, 211

Food taxes, 140

Foreign countries, 135

Foreign securities, 198

Foreign trade, 161

Foreigner made to pay, 127-128, 131, 134

Friction, 36

Germany, war-made capital, 187

Graduation, policy of, 9, 89, 106, 248

Grants in Aid, 240, 250

Harcourt, Sir William, 8

Health, 71

Hereditary fortunes, 118

Houses, advantage of owning, 35; inhabited, 119; taxability, 30

Housing, 197; as index of income, 248

Imperial and local taxation, 228, 237

Imperial Preference, 141

Import tariff, 128, 235, 236

Import trade, 198; United Kingdom for 1913, 139-140

Imports, tariff on, 8

Incidence of taxation, 10, 66

Income, current, 10; definition, 13; distinction between costs and surplus, 26; earned and unearned, 95; general tax, 84; large, 93, 152; large, unearned, 155; taxation of, 78

Income tax, 7, 234; effect of raising, 157; local, 247; low-ering the limit, 48; progressive, 88; reforms, 95

Indirect taxation, 8, 49, 61, 121, 136, 140, 235

Individual returns of income, 109

Industrial Councils, 37

Industry, penalizing, 208-209

Inflation, 171

Inhabited House Duty, 119

Inheritance taxes, 8

Initiative, 24

Inland Revenue Commissioners, 88; tables of income tax progression, 90, 91

Interest, 95; minimum rate, 18

Land, economic rent, 27; values and improvements, 29

Land values, 246; difficulty and injustice of taxing only, 79; taxability, 31

Landed interests, 173

Landlords, 28; municipal improvements and, 242

Lawrence, Pethick, 189

Lawyers, 98

Levy on capital, 163, 165; arguments for, 196; general levy, 189; instalments, 223; objections answered, 191; two forms, 189, 224

Licence duties, 121

Life Insurance policies, 100

Liquor trade, 172

Local and imperial taxation, 228, 237

Local economic surplus, 245

Local income-tax, 247

Local rating, 245, 248, 250, 252

Local services, 241

Localism, 238

London money-market, 158, 215-216

Luxuries, 58, 119; general tax on, 124; taxes on, 120

Managers, high-salaried, 97

Manufactures, 141, 142, 159, 161

Marshall, Professor, 33
Minimum wage, family, 47
Money, Sir L. C., 170
Monopoly, 32, 38, 132; accidental, 112; economic, 30; limits, 39; state, 230
Motor cars and cycles, 58, 121
Municipal finance, 238
Munitions, 34

National debt, 146; *See also* War debt
National supervision, 239
National welfare, 72
Natural selection, 138
Necessities, absolute, 55
New York, 159, 216

Physiocrats, 28
Pigou, A. C., 151, 204
Post-war expenditures, 6
Preferential gains, 112
Prices, present and future, 181, 182; rise, 5
Professional incomes, 41, 97, 204; taxable capacity, 42
Profit, definition, 21; war, legitimate and illegitimate, 185
Profiteering, 166, 174, 177, 178; special committee on, 228
Profiteers, 97
Progression, Zorn's method, 92
Protective tariff on imports, 8
Psychology, 98
Public business, 70
Public services, 3

Quasi-rent, 33

Raid on capital, 210, 214
Reconstruction, 4
Reforms, 95
Rent, 27; increase, 242
Rents of ability, 40
Repudiation, 214
Restraint of trade, 126

Revenues, future, 6; public, 4, 229
Ricardo, 27
Rights of workers, 17
Rowntree, Mr., 47

Saving, 19, 68, 70, 96, 100; high taxation and, 157; public, 77
Savings, 113, 186; preferential treatment, 114; recent records, 168; remission on new saving, 115
Scammel, Herbert, 122
Scott, Professor, 202, 215
Scrapping present system, 46
Securities in exchange for war loans, 220, 222
Share distribution, 175
Shifting process, 13, 45
Shipowners, 171, 175
Short-time rent, 34
Single-tax, 79
Single-taxer, 28, 31, 79
Sinking fund, 163, 202
Smith, Adam, 27
Society, 73
Special levy on capital, 11
Specific taxes, 9
Stamp, J. C., 103, 180, 190
Stamp duties, 122, 125
Standard wage, 15
Standardized form of account, 108
State, 74; citizens' relation, 104; services and revenues, 228
State expenditure, future need, 5; increase in prospect, 4
State Socialism, 38
Stocking, 19, 21
Subsistence wage, 14
Sugar, 122
Super-tax, 91, 107
Supplementary taxes, 118
Surplus, ability to bear tax, 45, 233; costs distinguished from, 26, 45, 67; detailed items, 81
Surplus-income, definition, 27

Tariff duties, defects, 137
Tariffs for revenue, 127
Taxability, 231
Taxable surplus, 12, 234, 236
Taxation, basis, 234; normal policy of State, 235; tendencies, 7; two negative conditions, 12; what it does, 9
Tea, 122
Thrift, 208-209
Tobacco, 59, 122
Trade depression, 202
Transfer of property, 125

Unemployment, 197
Universal income-tax, 47

Valuables, 219
Valuation, 217, 227, 249
Value, 73
Values, fresh, 111

Wages, incidence of tax on, 50; standard wage, 15; subsistence wage, 14; tax policy, 15.
Wages of ability, 43.
War, effects in tariff policy, 141.
War debt, 146, 183; reduction, 148, 160, 183
War finance, 193
War loans, 191
War profits, 169
War taxation, experience, 60, 62
Wealth, growth of untaxed, 175; production, 73, 74; social not individual creation, 73; war-made, 165, 179
Webb, Sidney, 86, 240
Women-workers, 57
Workers, 14, 61
Working-class incomes, 103

Zorn, J., 92

CPSIA information can be obtained
at www.ICGtesting.com
Printed in the USA
BVHW031414171019
561388BV00001B/86/P